Tyranny of the Moment

Tyranny of the Moment

Fast and Slow Time in the Information Age

Thomas Hylland Eriksen

Pluto  Press

LONDON • STERLING, VIRGINIA

First published 2001 by Pluto Press
345 Archway Road, London N6 5AA
and 22883 Quicksilver Drive,
Sterling, VA 20166–2012, USA

www.plutobooks.com

British Library Cataloguing in Publication Data
A catalogue record for this book is available from the British Library

ISBN 0 7453 1775 8 hardback
ISBN 0 7453 1774 X paperback

Library of Congress Cataloging in Publication Data
  Eriksen, Thomas Hylland.
  Tyranny of the moment : fast and slow time in the information age /
Thomas H. Eriksen.
    p. cm.
  ISBN 0–7453–1775–8 (cloth) — ISBN 0–7453–1774–X (pbk.)
   1. Information society. 2. Information technology—Social aspects.
  3. Time—Social aspects. 4. Time pressure. 5. Computers and
  civilization. I. Title.
   HM851 .E75 2001
   303.48'33—dc21

                                                              2001003084

10   9   8   7   6   5   4   3   2

Designed and produced for Pluto Press by
Chase Publishing Services, Fortescue, Sidmouth EX10 9QG
Typeset from disk by Stanford DTP Services, Northampton
Printed and bound in the European Union by
Antony Rowe, Chippenham and Eastbourne, England

Contents

List of Figures

Preface

This book began with an uncomfortable feeling, which had grown steadily over the past few years and refused to go away. It seemed that this vague discomfort indirectly tried to tell me that something was about to go terribly wrong. The last couple of decades have witnessed a formidable growth of various time-saving technologies, ranging from advanced multi-level time managers to e-mail, voicemail, mobile telephones and word processors; and yet millions of us have never had so little time to spare as now. It may seem as if we are unwittingly being enslaved by the very technology that promised liberation. Concomitantly, the information revolution has led to a manifold increase in the public's access to information, which affects hundreds of millions worldwide, certainly including everyone who reads these lines; we enjoy, or suffer from, an availability of information that was unthinkable a generation ago. Yet the incredible range of information freely or nearly freely available has not created a more informed population, but – quite the contrary – a more confused population.

This double paradox, along with a nagging suspicion that changes which ostensibly boost efficiency and creativity may in fact do the exact opposite, is the starting-point for the exploration that follows. There are strong indications that we are about to create a kind of society where it becomes nearly impossible to think a thought that is more than a couple of inches long. Tiny fragments – information lint – fill up the gaps, invade coherent bodies of knowledge and split them up, and seem certain to displace everything that is a little old, a little big and a little sluggish. People in their fifties find it difficult to sell themselves in the labour market unless they masquerade as young, dynamic, open-minded and flexible people. Nothing is more hopelessly dated than last week's fashion. And so on. I am no romantic or Luddite – like everyone else, I am impatiently waiting for a decent company to offer me a superfast, cheap and stable Internet connection – but it is impossible to applaud the current drift towards a society where everything stands still at enormous speed.

In 1999 I was on a sabbatical from my job at the University of Oslo. For some reason I did not get much research done, but I did

work diligently and indeed got a lot of desktop clutter out of the way
– articles, proofs, reports, e-mails... Whenever I had cleared my desk,
I might go down the corridor to fetch a cup of coffee, and just as I
opened the door to re-enter the office, the mess had already begun
to reappear. Eventually there was no option other than to sit down
calmly to analyse how it could be that it seemed completely
impossible to work continuously and slowly with a major project (at
last, then, I got some research done, namely on why I couldn't get
any research done). The short answer is that there were always so
many other little tasks that had to be undertaken first that I never
got going with the slow, tortuous work that is academic research.
This realised, I began to write what eventually grew into the present
book, which exposes and criticises some unintended consequences
of information technology. Given the topic, there is a danger that
the book will be filed under cultural conservatism or, worse, cultural
pessimism. That would be very far from my intentions. As in my
previous work (most of which is unknown outside of Scandinavia),
I still hold cosmopolitan, anti-nationalist, politically radical views;
I am convinced that cultural and political globalisation may
ultimately lead to a truly global humanism, and I also believe that
'new work' – the style of work typical for information society – is an
advance on the routine drudgery and rigid hierarchies dominating
industrial society. *Tyranny of the Moment* does not, in other words,
intend to give voice to yearnings for a society without the Internet,
a nostalgic longing for rusty factory gates or, for that matter, the
sturdy pleasures of the agrarian life, or any other view of the generic
'stop the world, let me off' type. The aim is not and cannot be to
abolish information society, but to create an understanding of its
unintended consequences.

The acceleration typical of information society has a long
prehistory with powerful reverberations through time. It is directly
connected with the telegraph and the steam train, and it increasingly affects most aspects of our lives – from family and style of
thought to work, politics and consumption. It can be described in a
thousand ways and, not least, on several thousand pages. My
motivation for treating the topic in a short book of this kind consists
in the possibility that it might make a difference – the aim, in a word,
is to contribute to a critical reflection about the kind of society we
are unwittingly creating. Over the last year I have given many talks
on the relationship between time, technology and human life, and
audience reactions have been mixed. People who work in the IT

sector or other service professions, including journalism and the bureaucracy, have generally reacted favourably to my descriptions of acceleration and hurriedness, confirming the assumption that their working days are overloaded, their leisure time is being chopped up, they are unable to work for a sustained period on a project, which in turn affects their family life, and so on. Others have been less enthusiastic. The very sensible manager of my children's kindergarten objects that it is impossible for her staff, and for others in similar professions, to reduce their working speed and stress level. A group of local politicians and NGO representatives reacted to one of my rather hurried and fact-laden talks by saying, by way of introduction, that 'listening to you is enjoyable' – I am used to this kind of mock flattery, and was by then waiting for the 'but' clause – and indeed, 'but this is only about a handful of people of your own kind, whose level of activity is unnaturally high'. Difficult objections to respond to? Not really. As this book hopefully shows, its topic is relevant to all of us.

A different version of this book was published in Norwegian by H. Aschehoug in spring 2001. In preparing the English version, I considered the possibility of trying to erase every visible trace of its Scandinavian origin, replacing all examples and all local flavour with UK or US equivalents. I soon thought better of it. Instead, I have opted for a compromise, replacing those Scandinavian examples which do not make sense out of context and thereby avoiding involuntary lapses into travel writing, but keeping others. Inviting an English-language readership to see the world in globalisation (or glocalisation) with Oslo as a vantage-point, just this once, will not do any harm. The issues are universal, and a Manhattan perspective is no less provincial than an Oslo perspective anyway.

Oslo, 2001
T.H.E.

1 Introduction: Mind the Gap!

0821: Scan the first page of *Aftenposten*, the Oslo broadsheet, while waiting for the traffic lights to change. A half-page advert entices readers with the one-liner: 'Watch Norway's fastest TV programme'. Thanks anyway.

0835: Buy a tabloid in the canteen. Got to have something to read while I'm waiting for the lift.

0843: Enter the office. Turn on the computer. 21 new e-mails since yesterday afternoon. Hang my coat on a peg and fetch coffee.

0848: Looking forward to starting to write. Just have to take the phone and check something on the web first.

0853: Cannot find the information I'm looking for. Start replying to e-mail instead.

0903: Understand, in a rare glimpse of genuine reflexivity, that something has to be done. Turn off the computer, pull out the phone cord and begin to take notes in longhand.

But this, I have to admit, is a misrepresentation. The last entry is anyway. Apart from the very first, fumbling notes made on a Palm handheld computer and on scraps of paper, this book is in its entirety written on a word processor. Like others who have grown up with the keyboard as their fourth finger joint, I have enormous problems writing anything more substantial than a postcard by hand. In reality, it happened like this: I had a few general ideas and keywords, some electronic notes from talks I had given, and a few one-liners I was pleased with. I then began to re-work the notes into a kind of continuous prose, while simultaneously trying out different outlines for the book as a whole. When the content of this initial document, after a frustrating period of abortive attempts and non-starters, cutting and pasting, adding and deleting, began to show the rudiments of a kind of linear progression, it was too long to be manageable (in my case, the limit is about 30 pages in 12 point, that is about 80,000 characters). I then divided the file into seven separate files, one for each main chapter. I wrote the draft version of Chapter 3 first, and then began work on Chapter 2. But then I painted myself into a corner, left Chapter 2 as a troll with three heads but no tail, and embarked on the middle section of Chapter 5 instead. While

1

writing, I continuously entered keywords and scattered ideas into the other open files. Until a very short time before the publisher's deadline, the whole manuscript was punctuated with lacunae, missing paragraphs, missing references, question marks and incomplete sentences.

In the old days, there was a rigid distinction between a draft and a finished text. When one began to copy out a manuscript, one ought to know where one was heading, irrespective of genre. Preferably, one should have a long, coherent line of reasoning or a well-structured plot present in the mind when one wrote the first sentence. When one had copied it out, the text was finished and went to a professional typesetter. This is no longer the case, as the above description indicates. Nowadays, writers work associatively, helter-skelter, following whims and spontaneous ideas, and the structure of a text is changed under way; the ship is being re-built at sea. Word processing has probably affected both thought and writing more than we are aware, but exactly how it has affected the way we deal with information has not yet been subjected to systematic scrutiny. Would a messy work of genius such as Marx's *Capital*, for example, have been shorter or longer, simpler or more complex if its author had had access to word processing software? It would, I suspect, have been tidier and less complex. Probably at least 25 per cent longer. Because of the very style in thought and writing word processing encourages, the chapters and 'books' that make up *Capital* would have seemed more like blocks stacked on top of each other than organic links in a long, interconnected chain of deeply con-centrated reasoning.

This is to do with time and technology, and the ways in which technology affects the way we live in time. These may seem large philosophical questions that ought to be treated with great deference and deep bows in the direction of Kant, Bergson and Heidegger. However, the issues have recently announced their arrival right at our doorstep by entering everyday life. The actual take-off of this new era was in the second half of the 1990s, and this will be demon-strated in later chapters. For this reason, the issues can and should be treated in a concrete and largely commonsensical way.

A central claim of the book is that the unhindered and massive flow of information in our time is about to fill all the gaps, leading as a consequence to a situation where everything threatens to become a hysterical series of saturated moments, without a 'before' and 'after', a 'here' and 'there' to separate them. Indeed, even the 'here and now' is threatened since the next moment comes so quickly that it becomes difficult to live in the present. We live with our gaze firmly fixed on a point about two seconds into the future. The consequences of this extreme hurriedness are overwhelming; both the past and the future as mental categories are threatened by the tyranny of the moment. This is the era of computers, the Internet, communication satellites, multi-channel television, SMS messages (short text messages on GSM phones), e-mail, palmtops and e-commerce. Whenever one is on the sending side, the scarcest resource is the attention of others. When one is on the receiving side, the scarcest resource is slow, continuous time. Here lies a main tension in contemporary society.

Allow me also to put it like this: as a boy, I belonged to that subculture among children whose members are passionately interested in space travel and dinosaurs. Only late in puberty did I realise that there were thousands upon thousands of children, spread thinly across the modern world, who had been in exactly the same situation as myself: they were bored by the tedious routines of school, they were below-average performers in sports, and were for these reasons easily tempted by various forms of imaginative escape from reality, frequently spending their days among knights and dragons in societies of the generic J.R.R Tolkien kind, or at recently founded space colonies in the Andromeda region or on the moon, or else in the no less marvellous universe of natural science and technology.

The popular science fiction literature directed at an adolescent readership of this generic kind depicted two complementary futures. One of them was abruptly called off in the mid-1980s. When the Challenger space shuttle exploded and the crew was killed in January 1986, an era was over – or, rather, a likely future had suddenly become extremely unlikely: the space age had been abolished. Today, more than 30 years after the Apollo XI, passenger shuttles to Mars are much further into the future (if there at all) than they were on that unforgettable summer day in 1969 when Neil Armstrong was the first human to set foot on the Moon.

The other future that was envisaged for us was the computer age. For most of those who grew up during the 1960s and 1970s, it seemed more remote, and much more abstract, than the space age. We were on friendlier terms with King Arthur, Frodo and Tyrannosaurus Rex than with Vax-I. Most of us had hardly even seen a computer, but we knew that they were enormous machines with a maze of thick wires and blinking bulbs, which required a large, sterile and air-conditioned room, a small army of engineers and a steady supply of punch-cards and paper strips to function. A few years earlier, the marketing director of IBM had uttered the immortal words, that the world needed a total of about ten computers.

From the late 1970s, microcomputers began to reach the consumer market, from producers such as Apple, Commodore and Xerox. In 1981, the 'PC' from IBM was launched in a major campaign aimed at a non-nerd market, and only three years later, Apple developed its first Macintosh, a computer equipped with a mouse and a graphic interface, both of which were later copied by Microsoft (and by a few other companies including Amstrad). An image which is very similar to the original Macintosh 'desktop' forms the display of most personal computers today. When IBM made their first major, ultimately ill-fated, assault on the market, computer gurus stated that within a few years, there would be a computer in every office, and many would even have one at home. People shook their heads in disbelief. A few years later there was a computer in every office, and many had one at home.

About ten years after the personal computer, the Internet had its major breakthrough. As I write, another decade has passed, and today it is easy to see that if one of our two complementary futures never delivered its goods, the other came with a vengeance: it arrived faster, and with much larger consequences, than anyone could have dreamed of a little more than two decades ago.

This is not a book about computers. They are far from irrelevant to the issues at hand, but blaming technology as such would be tantamount to shooting the pianist. The book is about information society and the strange social and cultural side-effects it has entailed, many of which are only obliquely related to computerisation. Economic growth and time-saving, efficiency-boosting technology may have made us wealthier and more efficient, and it may have given us more time for activities of our own choice, but there are sound reasons to suspect that it also – maybe even to a greater degree – entails the exact opposite. More flexibility makes us less flexible, and more choice makes us less free. Why do most of us have less time to spare than before, contrary to what one might expect? Why does increased access to information lead to reduced comprehension? Why are there no good, politically informed visions for the future in a society infatuated with the present and the near future? And why do we still feel that the loading of Microsoft Word takes too long? The answers are to do with too much complexity of the wrong kind and the increased rate of turnover in the rhythm of change.

There are several good reasons to be pleased about living right now (and certainly a lot of bad reasons). We live longer, we have a wider range of opportunities and, on the whole, more options than earlier generations did. This is particularly true of the rich countries, but there have been advances in this direction in many 'Third World' countries as well. Both longevity and literacy rates rose dramatically in most countries during the twentieth century, the current setbacks in Africa notwithstanding. Yet, something is about to go awry. That is our topic. Let me nevertheless stress – in case it should still be unclear – that the author is neither an old-fashioned romantic nor a nostalgic who dreams of a pre- or early modern age when coherence and wholeness could still be taken for granted. My relationship to new information technology is in principle active and enthusiastic, and I regard the information age as a worthy successor to the industrial age. How these views can be reconciled with a fundamental critique of a prevalent pattern in our age, I shall have to indicate in the course of the book, chiefly in the final chapter. The reader is not encouraged to cheat and check the contents of the last chapter first. This cellulose product is true to just that cultural style which is threatened: it is linear and cumulative. It has a particular, non-random order, and the chapters are not merely blocks stacked on top of each other; they are connected organically. The book thus gives the impression of having been written in a particular sequence; it imitates the era before word processing. The topic is of current interest, but the form – the slowly unfolding, reasoning essay – may well be judged as old-fashioned by the next generation of information consumers.

The story about the tyranny of the moment is about to begin, with a short overview of some characteristics of this era, the period after the Cold War. This era came about so fast that the best research still consists in trying to catch up with the present. The following chapter pursues some selected paths back in cultural history, emphasising the history of information technology and not least its unintended consequences. The fourth chapter introduces a particularly important aspect of the history of the last century or so, namely acceleration: nearly everything changes faster and faster, and we are only millimetres away from the point where a new product is obsolete before it hits the shelves. Time is hacked up into such small pieces that there is hardly anything left of it. The fifth chapter calls attention to a particular kind of mathematical function, namely exponential growth. The main property of exponential curves is the doubling of their values at regular intervals; so long as the numbers are small, they do not seem to grow dramatically. Eventually, they take off and begin to resemble vertical lines, which indicates – since the x axis represents time – that time approaches zero. Surprisingly many such curves can be identified nowadays. In the sixth chapter, I discuss a curious side-effect of acceleration and exponential growth, namely the phenomenon I call *stacking*: the strange fact that more and more of everything is stacked on top of each other rather than being placed in linear sequences. A couple of examples are information as funnelled through multi-channel television and the World Wide Web, but there are other, less obvious cases which may be no less consequential. The next and penultimate chapter shows what all this implies for everyday life in our kind of culture; how contemporary mores, ranging from serial monogamy and the cult of youth to 'flexible work' and new consumption habits can be seen as expressions of the tyranny of the moment.

In spite of its popular style and modest length, this is not an unambitious book. We are talking about nothing less than a new pattern, a new code and a new set of organising principles that may be about to dominate our kind of society. For that reason, it seems pertinent that it should end with some political considerations. It would be both simplistic and misleading to conclude that 'we must regain control over time'; instead I suggest that we must re-learn to value a certain form of time. In order to discover what this kind of time is like, in which domains it rightly belongs, why it is important and why it is threatened, there is no other solution I can think of than setting a few slow hours aside to read the entire book in a linear, cumulative fashion.

2   Information Culture, Information Cult

The phrase 'information age' has been around for some years now. It might well have been coined by Alvin Toffler when he wrote his bestselling books about future shocks and third waves in the 1970s, but as a concept it can be traced to media theorists like Marshall McLuhan, who wrote his most important books in the early 1960s, and further back to the cultural critics of the Frankfurt School, notably Adorno and Marcuse, presenting their apocalyptic visions for Western civilisation to grateful audiences of masochistic students in the years following the Second World War. It is no coincidence, however, that the term (and concept) of the information age had its major breakthrough in the 1990s. Like other fashionable terms, including globalisation and identity, the term easily becomes meaningless in the mouths of politicians, who may be tempted to use it in a rather glib way to prove that they are abreast with the current situation, not in order to say anything substantial about the differences between this kind of society and the industrial society, or 'mechanical age', which preceded it. It is a sad fact that perfectly good words become useless clichés just when they are needed the most; the reason is that these words tend to say something important about the present and are therefore appropriated by everybody. On the other hand, the falling marginal value of words – their decreasing value and shortened lifespan – is itself a symptom of the problems typical of information society.

Put differently, the phrase 'information society' has lost its meaning because of information society. The latter is a reality, and if one is going to make a serious attempt at understanding the contemporary age, there are a lot less useful ways to begin than by looking at the transition from industrial to informational society.

It should nevertheless be kept in mind that the last couple of decades have seen a great number of other changes as well, many of them pulling in the same direction – towards greater complexity, uncertainty and individualism. In 1980, there was not a single Indian restaurant in Oslo. In 2000 there were more than half a dozen within less than 10 minutes' walking distance from a flat I used to live in, ranging from fast food ('Curry & Ketchup') to a non-smoking, vegetarian Hare Krishna place and one offering five-star gourmet fare. In Douglas Adams's novel *Dirk Gently's Holistic Detective Agency* from 1988, the hero is exasperated at the lack of pizza delivery services in Oslo. This would not be a problem now; if anything, the problem consists in choosing between pizzas, Chinese, Indian and other cuisines available for home delivery via phone or the Internet. Everywhere in the rich countries, video recorders and personal computers have, during the last couple of decades, become as common as television became a little earlier. Bank branches have been closed down or re-designed with a view to keeping customers out; the personal cheque is becoming an obsolete means of payment, and Internet banking is rocketing upwards. Internet chat and SMS messages (short text messages transmitted between mobile phones) are becoming standard means of communication among teenagers. Until mid-1999, the SMS (Short Message System) technology for GSM phones was virtually unknown; it was initially meant to notify people that they had voicemail. It was then discovered by young people, who began to use the inexpensive service to keep in touch. The number of SMS messages sent in Norway in October 2000 was of the same order as the numbers sent in all 1999, indicating a twelve-fold increase in a year.

THE TWENTY-FIRST CENTURY BEGAN IN 1991

These anecdotal examples are naturally mere ripples on the surface, but they are connected to deeper structural changes. As a matter of fact, such changes make it not only possible, but necessary to state, without any further ado, that the twenty-first century began, not in 2000 or in 2001, but in 1991. This perhaps idiosyncratic view is indirectly supported by none other than Eric J. Hobsbawm, whose 'short twentieth century' begins in 1914 and ends in 1991.

This periodisation may be substantiated through three major global events which took place around 1991. The first was the breakdown of the Soviet Union. As a result politics, as we used to know it, disappeared. When there were still two superpowers more or less dividing the world between them, there was also a clear, visible distinction between left and right in politics. The USA represented an ideology based on a lot of individual freedom and little security (so little, actually, that a large proportion of the country's inhabitants owned handguns in order to be able to kill persons who threatened them). The Soviet Union represented its opposite – a great deal of security and very little personal freedom (so little, in fact, that one could be sent to a labour camp in Siberia if one spoke one's mind). The contrast between these two systems was translated into a series of related dichotomies; state versus free initiative, community versus individual, solidarity versus selfishness, and so on. Although there were very, very few in the West who earnestly liked the Soviet system (H.G. Wells may have been the last intellectual to do so; Sartre defended it on purely strategic grounds), it embodied an alternative way of organising human life, another view of human nature and another view of social planning than that which was prevalent in the USA. Most political movements in the world tried to position themselves between the extreme individualism of the USA and the extreme collectivism of the USSR; seen through the eyes of their detractors, these opposites marked the boundaries of a wide space for political debate. Long before Blair and Giddens, there were many 'third ways' actively being promoted around the world, ranging from Swedish-style social democracy to anarchism, Indian protectionism and Yugoslav economic democracy. The plethora of political alternatives that grew within the predictable, but frightening space created by the Cold War, all but vanished when one of the superpowers disappeared. As a result, the values embodied by the USA have become globally hegemonic. Ideology in the 1990s has largely been unself-conscious, the sound of one hand clapping.

The other major event was the dissolution of Yugoslavia and the ensuing wars. The tragedies of the Balkans in the 1990s were an indirect reminder that ethnic nationalism and fundamentalism could be a very strong countervailing force to the US hegemony and globalisation, at least in the short term. The wars also revealed a fact that researchers had been aware of for some time, namely that modernity does not lead to the disappearance of ethnic and other 'primordial' identities; on the contrary, identification based on kinship and place can be strengthened as an indirect result of increased education, more television channels and so on. These and other forms of 're-traditionalisation' are not uncommon reactions when people see themselves as being victimised and excluded by globalisation.

Further, the dissolution of Yugoslavia showed that collective identities are not given once and for all, and that the sovereignty and indivisibility of the state cannot be counted on in the future. One of the post-war dogmas in the study of international relations has been that changes of national boundaries could not be accepted. The case of Yugoslavia showed in dramatic ways that there is a great demand for communities that are both larger and smaller than those offered by existing states. In this, the identity discourses and ethnic conflicts in Yugoslavia are comparable to the uncertainties and shifting of identities presently characteristic of the USA and Western Europe, as well as tensions between purism (or fundamentalism) and mixing (or hybridity) among minorities. To this issue I shall return later.

Finally, the wars in the Balkans were among the first in a long line of wars without obvious good guys and bad guys. As late as the 1980s, humanists and moralists in the West could easily take a stance regarding wars in far-flung places. Usually, they would support struggling liberation movements and small peoples against oppressive states and superpowers. But who did the same humanists support during the civil war in Somalia? Who did they sympathise with in Rwanda; the Hutus or the Tutsis? And what is their view of the ongoing civil war in Sri Lanka? Even in the case of Israel/Palestine, there was considerably more ambivalence during the 1990s than had earlier been the case.

Not to mention the Gulf War, which broke out in January 1991 and which was famously described by Jean Baudrillard as a war that never really took place, but which was broadcast in daily instalments to the world, courtesy of CNN. The Gulf War marked the inauguration of the USA's 'new world order', confirmed nearly a decade later in the NATO campaign against Milosevic's Yugoslavia, where there was not one 'left-liberal' view, but at least two: about half of the European left was all for the military operations, the other half was against them. In the strange post-Cold War era that followed the evaporation of global bipolarity, strange bedfellows are being made continuously, as when *The Economist* strongly advised the UN to lift sanctions against Iraq for humanitarian reasons – an opinion that would formerly have been associated with anti-NATO and socialist views.

THE INTERNET IS A TEMPLATE FOR THE TWENTY-FIRST CENTURY

The third major event that may be located to 1991 is more directly relevant to the theme of this book and will accordingly be treated more thoroughly – although the collapse of politics, identity as a

scarce resource and geopolitical ambiguity are certainly also consti-
tuting features of the world of the twenty-first century.

The Internet had existed as a military communication network
since the late 1960s, until 1983 as ARPANET, but it was a closed
circuit eventually including, apart from military staff, academics and
networks of computer enthusiasts who exchanged games and information through so-called BBSs (electronic bulletin boards). It was
only around 1991 that the Internet became commercialised and
thoroughly civilianised, so that Mr and Mrs Smith could get an
Internet account at home; and it was around this time that even
European academics began to use e-mail routinely.

A couple of years later, the World Wide Web, that graphic interface
which to many people *is* the Internet, was launched. My first
encounter with the web took place in the spring semester of 1993,
when one of our computer engineers called on me to update my
software. Employees at the University of Oslo had already been using
e-mail for a couple of years by then, but most of us only had vague
notions of other uses for this emerging global network.

The computer man double-clicked on an icon called 'Mosaic 1.0'.
'This is something new called the World Wide Web', he explained,
and added, switching to a prophetic mode: 'It's going to be
enormous.' He ran through the underlying principles – 'URL', 'http',
'graphic interface', 'HTML' – and then went on to show me a few
web sites. The University of Adelaide and the Library of Congress
were two of them. Oh well, I thought, so here one may eventually
find reading lists from Southern Australia and inventories from the
world's largest library. Is this progress? 'There isn't that much out
there yet', the computer man said apologetically, 'but just wait.'

The rest is, as we say, history. Already in the autumn of the same
year, the density of web sites (or 'home pages') began to increase
noticeably. The computer companies established their sites, other
companies such as record labels and publishers followed; most major
and quite a few minor universities and colleges went online, with
improved layout and thicker content from one week to the next. The
then extremely trendy California magazine *WIRED* wrote in 1994
that the coolest thing to do this week, was to make one's own home
page. Many did. At the same time, a thick undergrowth of websites
devoted to arcane topics began to flourish: anarchism, progressive
rock, science fiction, religious sectarianism... The large and the small,
the mainstream and the underground; they all went on to the web

during the 1990s, adding in no small measure to the acceleration and stacking of information typical of our age.

The WWW took off nearly immediately. New, improved versions of the web 'mark-up language' HTML and related advances, including Java, a new programming language for the web, made it possible to include sound, animations, any kind of formatted text, reply coupons and so on. The transmission speed or bandwidth increased and continues to do so. Nobody knows just how many million web pages exist out there this month, but at the time of writing, the number of sites is approaching 100 million. Each site contains anything between one and a huge number of pages.

The WWW represents something qualitatively new. The web can perhaps, in the words of author William Gibson, be compared to a never-ending journal, or a large library, but it is distinct from a library even if we do not take the amount of advertising into account. Above all, information on the web is not ordered, either alphabetically or in any other way. Different topics are linked together according to varying, often whimsical principles. The web is not hierarchical either, and a site belonging to a skilled student can be just as attractive, and take just as much space on the screen, as Microsoft's home page.

In other words, the web is incredibly democratic and decentralised, and this must be the main reason why the powers that be take such great pains to try to regulate it. As is well known, pornography of all kinds exists in large amounts there; if one looks, one will also find political propaganda and hate speech of every kind, exhortations to break the law, eccentric utterances and – naturally – terabytes of advertising. Some pessimists fear that the web will degenerate to just another arena for marketing; they are, fortunately, wrong. Like the old media based on wood pulp, the web can up to a certain point be seen as a mere medium, an empty vessel that can be filled with practically everything. However, it also contributes to shaping the content. It is a much *faster* medium than, say, a leather-bound volume of Stoic philosophy. Contrary to McLuhan's view, the medium is not the message, but the medium does *shape* the message. The history of philosophy does not just *look* different on a CD-ROM, or in the shape of a novel or a film, from a 500-page book with no illustrations or, for that matter, hyperlinks. It *is* different. It may not be true that certain thoughts can only be worked out in German (as some Heidegger specialists seem to believe), but certain thoughts are longer than a web page and are necessarily interlinked with other thoughts in a sequential way and not through hyperlinks.

Further, unlike print media, content on the web changes continuously. Self-respecting companies no longer merely have web sites; they are about to *improve* their web sites. There can be no guarantee that a page that was available yesterday will be available today. Links must be updated monthly. Change is not a state of emergency, but a feature of everyday life.

The number of Internet users has grown very fast (see Figure 2.1). At the end of 2000, nearly 400 million people were online. Their geographical distribution is truly global – there are Internet users in every country – but skewed along the familiar lines. The number of Internet users in a given country nevertheless varies along dimensions other than material standard of living (unlike the distribution of private cars). In Norway, half the population (2.3 million) were online in 2000. Only three years earlier, the number was just half a million. All of Africa had slightly more Internet users than Norway (and a population that was more than 100 times larger), but if one subtracts relatively technologically advanced South Africa, there are less than half as many Internet users in the entire African continent than in one of the smallest European countries.

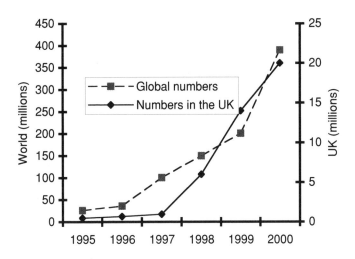

Source: www.nua.ie

Figure 2.1 Number of Internet users, 1995–2000

The most 'wired' countries in the world are the USA, Canada and the Nordic countries, where roughly half of the population had Internet access at the end of 2000. In Britain, about 35 per cent have access to the Net (in 1997, the figure was 2 per cent), while both Slovenes (25 per cent) and Estonians (22 per cent) are actually more online than the French (15 per cent).

It is still being said that 'nobody' makes money off the web, but the expectations remain high. In the winter of 1998/99, the Internet bookshop Amazon.com had a price-tag that was roughly equivalent to the total value of a medium-sized Scandinavian city like Trondheim. Although the nominal value has fallen since then, it is still astronomical, considering the company has yet to earn money and has little of value to sell in case of bankruptcy. Like most Internet-based companies, its chief asset is expectation.

IN INFORMATION SOCIETY, EVEN THE PIGS ARE IT COMPATIBLE

Information society is not the same as 'post-industrial society', which some talk about – a society where the main product is information, not industrial or agricultural products. In the USA, which – if anything – is an information society, traditional industry still represents more than half of the GNP. This is also the case in Germany, and in Japan, Toyota remains a more important cornerstone for the economy than Sony.

On the other hand, information society is characterised by the integration of information technology as a key factor in all kinds of production. Supermarket cashiers are totally dependent on computer technology; if the optical bar code reader collapses, they are helpless, especially since they no longer know the prices by heart. Greenhouses, milking machines and feeding machines for pigs are run by microprocessors. Indeed, the mating procedure for cattle is now entirely computerised in several countries; the coupling of cow and semen takes place via the Internet by way of a large database, and the semen is distributed in a frozen state from central stores. The physical bull is no longer required. It should come as no surprise, then, that the anxieties associated with possible computer breakdown at the transition from 1999 to 2000 (the 'Y2K' syndrome) were particularly widespread – not among writers, accountants and other regular computer addicts – but among European farmers. Whether one is about to blast a mountain, build a ship, sell a bag of crisps, investigate a case of arson, perform a heart bypass operation or give a lecture in social anthropology, people in our kind of society are increasingly dependent on computer technology. This is why the Y2K problem became such a powerful myth during 1999. Although many had a gut feeling that things would work out well, the myth of imminent breakdown was such a fantastic story about the vulnerabilities of the contemporary world that it was occasionally able to rival Clinton and Scary Spice as headline fodder. Suppose all mainframe computers broke down, what would happen then? Well, the pigs would be fed at erratic times and/or in strange quantities, lifts would stop between floors, microwave ovens would drop dead and ATMs would no longer be able to distinguish between deposits and withdrawals. Some even foresaw a situation where the only reliable thing in society would be ... the computers, since all serious software for microcomputers had been checked and double-checked for Y2K compliancy well before the great transition.

A modern myth tells of a man who had invented a sensational new weapon, an instrument which killed nobody, destroyed no buildings or even windows; all it did was to destroy paper. (A humanistic weapon it was – the opposite of the neutron bomb.) The bureaucrat in the patent office was sceptical, and advised him to go home and think it over before applying for a patent. The inventor nevertheless persisted, and finally the bureaucrat said, wearily: 'All right then, take that form and fill it in, and then go home.' The inventor quipped, triumphantly: 'You see?'

The Y2K myth is a variation of this story.

Apart from permeating the production of goods and services, information has grown steadily in importance as raw material. Of course, information has always been important, and, in a certain sense, every society is an information society. Anyone who knew how to kill a mammoth efficiently and (reasonably) safely, or how to make a fire without live embers, was a powerful person around the last Eurasian Ice Age. Yet it is a fact that there has been a shift towards information as the main scarce resource in the economy recently. Traditional raw materials have fallen in relative value; added value increasingly consists of information. For example, the cost of raw materials accounts for only 2 to 3 per cent of the value of a microprocessor. The rest is information. The most successful company in the world during the 1990s, namely Microsoft, makes its profits off products that can be transported electronically in packages with a weight of less than 1 gram. The Microsoft of the previous generation was called General Motors. Their packages had a gross weight of 4 tonnes.

A more familiar aspect is the fact that a growing part of the working population spend most of their time processing information. This is self-evidently the case with people who make a living talking, writing and reading, and our numbers have grown rapidly during the last decades. However, even today, academics, web designers, copywriters and journalists make up only a small proportion of the population in any country. The proliferation of 'information consultants' has been explosive in the 1990s, but there are still more farmers than information consultants in every country. On the other hand, many farmers in Western Europe work part-time as teachers or local government employees, and thus process pure information part of their working time. Information-related work sneaks into the working hours of groups who formerly used their time in other ways, sometimes simply as noise. A growing number spend a growing amount of their time in meetings, responding to telephone calls, faxes and e-mails; writing, reading, filing or destroying minutes from meetings, filling in forms, writing reports and so on. A report from the Norwegian equivalent to the National Health Service revealed that in the mid-1990s, an astonishing 60 per cent of the total budget of the national health service was spent on various forms of information processing. Computer specialist (and science fiction author) Jon Bing commented: 'The figure ought to have been, say, 4 or 5 per cent', but he added that nobody knew how to get there.

Information can be described as the driving force of the present Western economy, and more and more of it is being channelled through the Internet. When America Online and Warner Brothers fused in 1999, it was in practice the Internet company AOL that took over the entertainment company WB, and not the other way around. Although the profits of AOL were minuscule by comparison with those of WB, its stock value was nearly twice as high.

IN INFORMATION SOCIETY, FREEDOM FROM INFORMATION IS A SCARCE RESOURCE

Even people who do not have a job affected by the accelerated rhythm of information processing are deeply affected by the new technologies, by virtue of being consumers and ordinary citizens.

Unlike in other kinds of society, life in information society is characterised by redundancy and noise: there is far too much information around, and there is certainly enough for everybody, unlike in industrial and other kinds of society, where people experienced real information shortages (as witnessed in common metaphors such as 'thirst for knowledge' etc.).

My father was born in the 1930s. He grew up in a working-class family with few books. When he first began to earn money as a film reviewer for the local paper during secondary school, he immediately started buying books, and quickly became adept at it. Whenever he walked into a bookshop, he invariably emerged after a while with a bag or two, went home in a very good mood, stuck most of the books into their appropriate alphabetical places in the shelf, sat down in an easy chair and began to read the first one. That kind of activity embodied his view of the enlightened, modern person as well as offering considerable personal enjoyment. Now, I was born in the 1960s. My parents were middle-class, and for reasons already mentioned, I grew up in a home with a rather good-sized library. I am also, by virtue of living in the information age, pickled in information. Whenever I walk through a large bookshop, therefore, I regard it as a respectable achievement to be able to spend at least half an hour there without buying anything. Wide-ranging browsing without buying indicates that the personal information filters are functioning. There is too much information, not too little. And the amount increases. The figures for submitted materials to the Norwegian national library, which for reasons of domestic politics is located in a remote and depopulated place near the Arctic Circle called Mo i Rana, include all publications, widely defined – films, books, magazines, postcards, CD-ROMs; that is, most non-electronic mass communication produced in Norway. Over the course of seven years in the 1990s, the number of titles submitted per year more than doubled, from 48,400 in 1991 to 100,008 in 1998. and this in a country with fewer than 5 million inhabitants.

A crucial skill in information society consists in protecting oneself against the 99.99 per cent of the information offered that one does not want (and, naturally, exploiting the last 0.01 per cent in a merciless way).

One of my favourite texts on the unintended consequences of information society was written three decades ago, by a writer who declined to take the leap to word processing until the mid-1990s. His name is Tor Åge Bringsværd (pronounciation roughly as in Italian; 'Å'

= the 'aw' in 'raw', 'æ' = the 'a' in 'man'), a prolific and highly regarded novelist in Norway, and the story is 'The man who collected the first of September 1973' (in the original, the year was 1972). It tells the story of a man who realises that there is too much information in the world. No matter how much he tries, he will never arrive at an enlightened overview of history, politics, science and so on. One day, he takes a momentous decision. He makes a vow to work intensively the coming weeks and months to obtain a full overview of this single day, 1 September 1973. That much, he reckons, he can handle. So he rolls up his sleeves and starts collecting. He buys all the Norwegian and Scandinavian newspapers, he orders recordings of radio broadcasts, then moves on to newspapers and other publications in foreign languages, and soon realises that he will need to take intensive courses in Russian and other important languages he does not know. After several years of collecting material, a fire destroys our hero's flat, which is by now filled to the brim with clippings, tapes and scrapbooks about 1 September 1973. From his hospital bed, our hero, who has suffered minor burns, babbles incoherently about President Nixon and Chairman Mao, reports from football games in late August 1973 and so on; and he is naturally diagnosed as a dangerous lunatic by the nurses.

A few years later, Bringsværd approached the topic from a different angle. In the opening sequence of his masterful, but untranslated novel *The Oversleeper's Sad Breakfast*, we encounter Mr Felix Bartholdy, standing outside a bookshop in New York with a heavy bag in his hand and a cashier's slip in his pocket. He considers the weight of the bag and makes some rapid calculations, while muttering, to passers-by: 'I have bought all this stuff this evening. *But can anyone tell me when the hell I am going to find time to read all of it?*'

Bartholdy continues, thinking aloud: 'I have more than 10,000 volumes already. About 4,000 of them are still unread. Usually, I read two books a week. Two books a week equals 104 books in a year. In order to plough through 4,000 volumes, I shall need around 40 years. I am 43 years old. Before I have finished readings the books I already *have* bought, I shall be 83. But that is not all...' – he begins to feel dizzy and leans against the wall as he concludes, whispering: 'I continue to buy. I stockpile. I grab everything I see. I am a sick man. I buy at least five times as many books as I read.'

As it happens, things only get worse for Felix Bartholdy, but he is a true-born child of his age; in a sense, he is a couple of decades ahead of his time (the novel was published in the mid-1970s). He lives in an era with no Internet or digital television, an era when a mere 550,000 books are published annually in the world (he is aware of this figure), compared with nearly twice as many two decades later. But he is a typical victim of information overload. Facing the enormity of an ocean of information, he does not learn to swim. Quite the opposite, he will not be satisfied until he has drunk the entire ocean.

LESS IS MORE

In the classic modern era, with its itinerant lecturers (women and workers were favourite target groups), socialist reading groups organised by trade unions and ambitious state programmes to 'educate the people' about anything from contraception to the dangers of smoking, it was a common notion that most people were in dire need of increased knowledge. For knowledge was power; at least, power over one's own conditions of life. This slogan is still valid, but there has been a major shift in that information is no longer scarce. The point is no longer to attend as many lectures as possible, see as many films as one can, have as many books as possible on the shelves. On the contrary: the overarching aim for educated individuals in the world's rich countries must now be to make the filtering of information a main priority.

In this situation of extreme informational redundancy, a person who wants to understand his or her society, culture or anything else, cannot aim at obtaining as much information as possible. That would be tantamount to reading two books simultaneously – the telephone directory for the whole world and a 10,000-volume dictionary – and begin, diligently, on the first page in both works. One would never be able to advance beyond Abrahamson and Amoeba, even if one went on for a lifetime. This is Felix Bartholdy's problem, and avoiding it may well be the most important human challenge in the information age.

It is sometimes said that our generation runs out of things our grandparents had never heard of. What we now seem to run out of, is lack of information.

In this situation, an acute need for a sorting mechanism appears. What are the criteria for distinguishing between good and bad, knowledge and noise, when the supply of everything is limitless?

How can I sleep at night knowing that I have filtered away 99.99 per cent of the information I have been offered; how can I be certain that the 0.01 per cent that I actually use is the most relevant bit for me, in so far as I haven't even sniffed at the rest?

In the old days, the answer to this kind of question was either a sound education (*Bildung*), a secure personal identity or distinct interests. Today, the jungle has become so dense that one needs to be both stubborn and single-minded in order to be well informed about anything at all. Even someone paid by the state to do research on, say, chaos theory, cannot possibly read everything that is being written within the field, even if one restricts the scope to the English-language literature. It is viable to scan titles, summaries and tables of contents into the brain, but continuous texts? Forget it. Other tasks are waiting. The next moment kills the present.

The need for filters, pathfinders, organising principles for knowledge becomes overwhelming. Or does it? Is it perhaps rather the case that growing numbers of people become accustomed to living in a world where colourful fragments of information flit by, lacking direction and cohesion – and do not see this as a problem? I suspect this is happening to many of us, and if such is the case, an unintended consequence of the information revolution may be a fundamental transformation of the notion of knowledge.

IN INFORMATION SOCIETY, THE GAPS ARE BEING FILLED WITH FAST TIME

Extrapolating from commonly available statistics, it is possible to state that the person who is reading this right now is more likely to eat cornflakes than porridge for breakfast, and that he or she is also more likely to skim a newspaper today than to read an entire journal article. It is more likely that the person in question has a mobile telephone than not, it is highly likely that he or she has grown accustomed to using both fax and e-mail, has an answering machine or voicemail at work and at home, and several times during the past week has pressed that lift button which makes the doors close a little earlier than otherwise. Suppose the net gain of pressing this button is 5 seconds at a time. Suppose, further, that one takes the lift four times a day, five fimes a week. This implies 100 seconds of saved time every week. In a month, one will have saved six and a half minutes, and during a year with perfect conditions, one will have saved more than an hour! What to do with this extra time? Allow me to make some suggestions:

- Relax with a computer game or a television programme.
- Wait for a delayed flight.
- Read five tabloids or a broadsheet thoroughly.
- Drive from London to Brighton.
- Jog.
- Talk to one's children about their future or with one's parents about their past.
- Learn ten Spanish verbs in all conjugations.

Of course, an hour can be used for anything. A list of this kind could easily have filled several volumes. It is impossible to say exactly which time this saved time is, since our mechanical, clock-driven time is empty and abstract. I still contend that the entire hour saved is, as a matter of principle, spent waiting for the lift, and the saved seconds are eaten at a frightful rate when one is waiting for a lift which insists on stopping on every floor before reaching the ground floor.

The density of time increases. The gaps are being filled. There is more and more of everything, and given this context, it does perhaps give us a particular satisfaction to feel that we can control our time budgets by pressing that little button in the lift, just as few office workers shed tears when they suddenly get a full hour as a present because a meeting has been cancelled. It has become easier for a lot of people to identify with Jean-Paul Sartre, about whom it has been said that he habitually wore moccasins to save the time he would otherwise have used tying his shoelaces.

In information society, the scarcest resource for people on the supply side of the economy is neither iron ore nor sacks of grain, but *the attention of others*. Everyone who works in the information field – from weather forecasters to professors – compete over the same seconds, minutes and hours of other people's lives. Unlike what happens to physical objects, the amount of information does not diminish when one gives it away or sells it. If Jim has two apples and gives one apple to Peter, he has one apple left. But if Jim has two ideas and gives one of them to Peter, he may well end up with three, since Peter probably adds his comments. Be this as it may, any enterprise which supplies knowledge or information has a warehouse that can never become empty. The goods can only become obsolete and unmarketable – the informational economy's equivalent to empty stores – and this happens all the time and at increased speed.

For people who live in this kind of society (sometimes identified by the outside world as 'customers'), the main scarce resource does not consist in, say, tables and chairs, smoked hams and stuffed buffalo heads (although such things are naturally sold and bought as before), but *control over our own time*. Information is forcing itself upon us from the outside, more aggressively and this is more difficult to resist than, say, stuffed buffalo heads. There is always more where it comes from. The war over the free seconds is on.

This is not just about WAP (Wireless Application Protocol) telephones and cordless access to the Internet. That is part of the picture, and it is important: these media are new, they grow at a terrific rate, and nobody knows exactly what the Net will look like, or how it will be used, in three, four or five years – or whether it will chiefly be accessed through television, hand-held computers or mobile phones, or via the desktop computer as is the case today. But information is epidemic and spreads across all fields. The last ten to fifteen years of the twentieth century saw not just the rise of the Internet and related technologies, but also considerable growth in voice telephony, books published and television channels.

NO TECHNOLOGICAL CHANGES TURN OUT AS ANTICIPATED

This is to do with the relationship between technology, society and culture. A lot can be said – and is being said – about this relationship; for now, we must restrict ourselves to stating that it is complex. It is both easy and tempting to reach simple conclusions about the 'effects' of technological innovations, be it the typewriter, television or something else. Such assumptions are always wrong: technological change always points in several possible directions. Most good science fiction writers, including brilliant visionaries such as William Gibson and J.G. Ballard, focus nearly exclusively on the *side-effects* of technology; how it is being exploited by criminals or evil people, or leads to cultural disasters, or changes the human mode of thought in ways nobody had predicted. These writers know their cultural history, and are aware that earlier technical changes led to other, often more dramatic, changes than the inventors had envisioned at the time.

Take, for instance, the telephone. Apart from the fact that some people regarded it as a toy with a limited practical applicability, few predicted that it would rapidly alter urban residential patterns. This is exactly what happened with respect to groups who depended on regular and frequent contact with colleagues, customers and others. Before the telephone became common among the middle class at the beginning of the twentieth century, professional politicians tended to live in certain neighbourhoods. This was practical, since an important part of their job consisted in coordination and lobbying outside office hours. Then they each got their telephone; suddenly they could live wherever they wanted, and many moved out of the city centres.

Another example is the typewriter. The first mechanical 'writing machine' was Malling's Writing Ball, invented by the Danish priest Hans Rasmus Johann Malling Hansen in 1867. Its main purpose was to make it easier for blind and visually impaired people to write. One of its early users was Friedrich Nietzsche, who suffered from poor eyesight. Some commentators have retrospectively gone so far as to argue that Nietzsche's brief, aphoristic, chopped-up 'late style' was a direct result of the new writing technology. Although this may be an exaggeration, he himself wrote in a letter dated 1882 that 'the writing implements affect our thoughts'.

Apart from its possible effects on thought and reasoning, the introduction of the typewriter revolutionised the production of texts in a matter of a short time. Armies of female secretaries became a standard image of efficiency in the matured industrial society, and publishing became faster and easier. Hitherto, typesetters had spent a great deal of time and energy deciphering hopeless handwriting. At the same time, the typewriter rendered texts more anonymous in character, and just as people may nowadays apologise for sending personal letters as e-mails, they had similar misgivings about using the typewriter in the same way then. And just as we may defend our exaggerated e-mail usage by referring to its speed and reliability, typewriter converts argued that they saved the recipient's eyes by avoiding illegible longhand.

The changes brought about or directly inspired by the typewriter were thus many. It brought women into offices in large numbers, it created distance between the writer and the text, it led to greater speed and precision in copying and typesetting, and – arguably – it led to changes in the mode of thought. The most important living theorist of speed, Paul Virilio, belongs to that select group of authors who insist on writing by hand. All his books are written by pen. Only thus can he reduce the speed of writing to match his rhythm of reasoning.

What are the side-effects of word processing? In the 1980s, before Windows and Word gradually erased the major differences between leading operating systems, Macintosh users and MS-DOS users were accustomed to very different ways of relating to their computers. (Anthony Burgess once got a Macintosh, but hesitated to use it because he found it debasing to write on an instrument that greeted him with a smile and a welcome when he turned it on.) The Macintosh display showed a stylised image of a desktop, and one used the mouse to click one's way around. In the word processor, the display was pleasantly black-and-white and WYSIWYG (What You See Is What You Get), with correct fonts, adjusted margins and so on. A classic MS-DOS PC, on the other hand, greeted its user with the more reserved statement 'A>', possibly 'C>' if one had a hard drive. The text was amber or green on a black background. The word processor, which was usually called WordPerfect, displayed only a sordid standard font; any added effects (such as Helvetica 12 points, adjusted right margin, line spacing 1.5) were visible only in the print-out. A study of North American college students from this period indicated that the PC users generally submitted better written work than Mac users. Since it was so easy to make typographically 'finished' products on a Mac, these students were seduced into believing that they were ready to submit their work long before it was actually finished. There were also indications to the effect that the kind of technology used also influenced choice of topics. While PC users delved into serious fields like law, politics and economics, Mac users preferred to write about personalities from the entertainment industry and sports events. A test panel of 13-year-olds had generally few problems in understanding the Mac texts, but could not penetrate the more complex language of the PC users. Unfortunately, the study does not solve the chicken-and-egg problem; that is to say, it does not reveal whether the Mac users were more childish and superficial (and, perhaps, more creative) than the PC users *before* they chose their writing technology.

The word processor takes the logic of the typewriter further. It reduces the inherent resistance in the technology even more, making the production of texts a painless matter (and thereby in its way contributing in no minor way to the information overload). It widens the gulf between the writer and the text, and shrinks the distance between writer and typographer.

Marx once wrote, infamously, that 'the hand mill creates a society with a feudal lord, while the steam mill creates a society with an industrial capitalist'. In this often quoted sentence, he seems to promote *technological determinism*, the belief that technological changes inevitably and automatically entail particular societal changes. Most of the writers who deal with these issues, including the later Marx, are more cautious. Technology has unintended side-effects, and it is always enmeshed in a cultural context where it is difficult to predict exactly how it will be used. There is thus good reason to be modest in one's generalisations about the consequences of, for example, the Internet and cheap air travel for the lived reality in the rich countries during the past decade. But going to the opposite extreme, and arguing that technological changes make no difference at all, would be just as silly as believing that the Internet immediately turns the world as we know it on its head. There are clear indications that the Net is already generating lasting and highly consequential changes, and the position defended in this book is closer to technological determinism than to its opposite. Techno-logical changes that are implemented in a wide range of instances, reduce flexibility in society as a whole and steer activities in particular directions. As the next chapter will show, a world without the clock, printing and money would have been an entirely different world from the one we live in; and the current revolutions in electronic communications are ultimately of the same order as these watersheds. You ain't, in other words, seen nothin' yet.

IN THE TWENTY-FIRST CENTURY, FREEDOM AND VULNERABILITY ARE SYNONYMS

The revolution in information technology is an integral part, and a driving force, of a more comprehensive process of change which gained momentum in the 1990s. This, the years immediately following the Cold War, has been an odd and often confusing period. Oblique. Difficult to understand. This is connected to the revolution in communications in at least two ways. The obvious link is to do with acceleration and stacking, which will be discussed at length later. The less obvious link is with the very establishment of the post-Cold War (dis-) order. Some actually argue that the disappearance of the Iron Curtain is directly connected with information technology, and this view deserves serious treatment. Given the new possibilities for communicating across borders, which were increasingly available in Eastern Europe during the 1980s, authoritarian governments found it difficult to control the flow of information in their countries. A one-sided, state-run propaganda apparatus is hardly compatible with two-way communication over the global telecom network. (A one-sided, commercial propaganda apparatus is clearly better equipped to meet the challenges of global communication.) Both access to external information and internal networking among dissident groups became easier and safer when the airwaves replaced wood pulp as a dominant medium. People all over Eastern Europe quickly learned about the opening of the Austro-Hungarian border in spring 1989, about the liberalisation of the Bulgarian Communist Party the same autumn, and about tendencies towards radical change in Gorbachev's Soviet Union. When the checkpoints of the Berlin Wall were opened on 9 November 1989, the East European regimes fell like so many dominoes, surprisingly fast.

The causes of the fall of 'Communism' are complex, and this is not the appropriate place for a detailed analysis. But there is little doubt that the *speed* of the regime changes has to be seen in the light of changes in information technology.

With the fall of the Wall, we have entered the 1990s, that is the early twenty-first century according to my timeline. Television, telephones and Internet connectivity are becoming rapidly more widespread everywhere (see Figure 2.2).

Only a few, curious states such as Burma and North Korea seriously try to protect their citizens against uncensored impulses from the outside. Youth gangs in Mauritius get into mischief, inspired by the *Rambo* films, while discontented groups everywhere get ideas for change by watching television reportage from Palestine and Northern Ireland. Ideas spread faster and faster. On the whole, people all over the world know more about each other than ever before, and the information on offer is changed daily. The scene changes fast, the stability and predictability of the Cold War are gone. The left/right divide in politics has become fuzzy. The resistance to immigration, for example, is just as strong in Europe's social democratic parties as on the traditional right. The left has in these years shown a tendency towards nostalgia and conservation, even if its historical task, for the past 200 years, has been to promote change. A concern with form and style rather than substance has

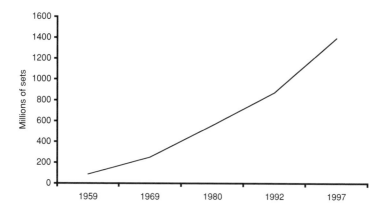

Source: Held et al. 1999, p. 358, www.unesco.org

Figure 2.2 Number of TV sets in the world, 1959–97

been symptomatic of politics in many countries during this period, and the actual differences between conservative and social democratic parties have become much less obvious than ever before. Political divisions follow lines that are not yet clearly demarcated, and the historical left is in search of a new, persuasive definition of its project.

The bipolar world has been replaced with a unipolar world. That pole is called market liberalism and individualism, and it beats the drum with catchwords like flexibility, freedom and openness. Resistance is scattered and uncoordinated. Access to information is not a scarce resource, but sorting mechanisms are.

Openness and pluralism are two ambiguous keywords describing the new era. Their connotations are positive in the dominant ideology, but the reality may well be different. One typical result of openness is uncertain identity. More and more people are uncertain as to exactly who they are looking at in the mirror in the morning. The nation is no longer what it used to be; to many, national identity is an obsolete way of talking about oneself. Gender seems relatively fixed, but no-one is able to state what it means to be a man or a woman any more – these roles change faster than sociology is able to monitor. Even age is no longer a reliable indicator of who one is, in an era when personal ads may well begin with the words, 'Boy, 40, seeks...'. The trade unions and the political parties have, in the space of a few years, become fuzzy entities that no longer offer people a safe home. New concepts of collective identities are regularly being launched, some of which seem to contradict the very idea that collectivities exist – nomadic, hybrid, urban, global identities. These labels need not be remembered; they are as ephemeral as the phenomena they describe.

The new era is liberating and frustrating, fascinating and frightening. It creates new forms of vulnerability: globally integrated computer networks imply that anything from computer viruses to designer drugs, lethal weapons and destructive thoughts flow more freely than ever before, bifurcate and result in incalculable effects through myriad butterfly effects. If the computers let us down, we are helpless – we cannot simply return to the feather pen, pretending everything is as it used to be. (In this way, the new 'flexibility' actually entails a loss of flexibility.) Further, it heralds the coming of a new *politics*, where the relationships between local and global forces, roots and impulses, traditional culture and a multi-ethnic reality set an agenda where there are no ready-made solutions available. It also creates a new *existential situation* for many people, who may (or have to) redefine themselves from day to day, in a context which lacks stability and predictability, where people are both free to choose and unfree not to choose. Further, the new era is, to many commentators, virtually synonymous with a new *economy*, that of 'new work' – information processing, flexibility and rapid turnover of firms, products and personnel being some of the catchwords. That there have been changes, and that these continue to make an impact, is obvious. When I grew up, Oslo had a large shipyard and three major breweries, and a valley north of the city centre (appropriately named Nydalen, 'New Valley', in the nineteenth century) had a motley mix of small and large factories, comprising some of the oldest industry in the country. Today, all of this (but one brewery) is gone, replaced by luxury flats, shops, restaurants, colleges, computer firms, book clubs, radio studios and so on. Last but not least, the new era is characterised by a continuous, dizzying and tiring flow of information which is just as rich in possibilities as it is poor in internal cohesiveness.

Information society can be described in thick books (this is naturally being done), but it can also be described like this: the point of gravity in the global economy has moved from things to signs. The sign economy changes at astonishing speed, and requires other organisational forms and a greater flexibility than the economy of things, since signs float more freely than things. It was ideas, not weapons, that ended up changing the regimes of Eastern Europe. Ideas and expectations also underpin the current economic boom in the West, as well as motivating rebellions and migration. The free availability of ideas simultaneously implies that many of them compete for the free spaces in our heads, leading to confusion and uncertain identities.

NEW TENSIONS SUPPLEMENT THE OLD ONES

Two revolutions characterise our age: the electronic and the multi-ethnic. In order to understand contemporary society it is not necessary to like either, but one has no choice but to admit that both are part of the air we breathe. Besides, they are two sides of the same coin. The electronic revolution and multi-ethnic society are mirror-images of each other: both disembed personal identity from tradition and roots, that is major, continuous narratives. The cultural mosaic typical of multi-ethnicity, with all its hybrid forms, paradoxes, conflicts and tensions, has its exact parallel in the fragmented, colourful, confusing and incoherent flood of information typical of multi-channel television and the World Wide Web. Both tendencies create flows, movement and unclear boundaries. They sever culture from place, people from ready-made stories about who they are and what they can become, work from the working place, consumption from routine, education from standard templates, knowledge from established models about what counts as knowledge... The past, wholeness, coherence – all of this is threatened.

The new conflicts that arise from information society can be depicted as a set of dichotomies, where the right-hand side dominates, while the left-hand side represents the counter-reactions.

familiarity	newness
security	freedom
communitarianism	liberalism
community	individual
roots	impulses
fundamentalism	ambivalence
past	future
continuity	change
maturity	youth

These kinds of tension fit badly within the right/left axis, and, as mentioned, 'radicalism' in the 2000s seems to be tantamount to resistance to change; the old left is worried about anything, from climatic changes to computer technology, multi-ethnic possibilities and urbanisation. We shall leave this matter here; there is in any case much to suggest that global social justice will be the overarching issue for a renewed left. In our context it is nonetheless relevant to take a quick look at the new forms of scarcity that emerge from information society. Some of them may be described like this:

slow time
security
predictability
belonging, stable personal identity
coherence and understanding
cumulative, linear, organic growth
real experiences (which are neither ironic nor mediated by mass media)

As Hegel correctly remarked, reality is always concrete. So if this seems abstract, I promise to go into a more experience-near mode very soon.

Still, some will argue that all this is not really new; all these themes, contradictions and problems are at least a hundred years old, in some cases as old as agriculture and urban society. As an answer to this kind of criticism, I have no better option than to offer an answer culled from the massive work of Manuel Castells, who writes, in a lengthy footnote towards the end of his three-volume *The Information Age*:

In discussions in my seminars in recent years a recurrent question comes up so often that I think it would be useful to take it to the reader. It is the question of newness. What is new about all this? Why is this a new world? I do believe that there is a new world emerging in this end of millennium. (...) Chips and computers are new; ubiquitous, mobile telecommunications are new; genetic engineering is new; electronically integrated, global financial markets working in real time are new; an inter-linked capitalist economy embracing the whole planet, and not only some of its segments, is new; a majority of the urban labor force in knowledge and information processing in advanced economies is new; a majority of urban population in the planet is new; the demise of the Soviet Empire, the fading away of communism, and the end of the Cold War are new; the rise of the Asian Pacific as an equal partner in the global economy is new; the widespread challenge to patriarchalism is new; the universal consciousness on ecological preservation is new; and the emergence of a network society, based on a space of flows, and on timeless time, is historically new.

He then comes up for air, and adds: *'Yet this is not the point I want to make. My main statement is that it does not really matter if you believe that this world, or any of its features, is new or not. My analysis stands by itself. This is our world, the world of the Information Age.'*

With this, the framework for an analysis of the tyranny of the moment should be roughly in place. But something important is still missing, and that is the relationship between technology, society and culture. The topic is very current, but one of my crucial points is going to be that it is impossible to understand the present without seeing it as the product of some relatively well-defined past – an insight which is both under serious assault in information society *and* misunderstood as an inducement to learn from history through miming or copying it. For this reason, the next chapter is pure cultural history, a series of snapshots from the history of information technology indicating some of the paths leading to the present. If this book, contrary to expectations, has some extremely hurried readers who would rather read about speed, growth and stacking, and what this means for you and me, it is strictly possible to skip the next chapter, but I discourage it, for reasons that should already be clear.

3   The Time of the Book, the Clock and Money

If all of evolutionary history, from the first single-celled organisms to the present with its anatomically modern elephants and humans (and, lest we forget, anatomically modern single-celled organisms), were to be compressed into 24 hours, modern humans arrived on the scene 5 seconds before midnight. The agricultural revolution appeared one and a half seconds before midnight. And the Internet? Forget it.

If this perspective is too dizzying, we may forget trilobites and brontosaurs for now, and limit the scope to the history of humanity seen as a day and night. That 24-hour cycle would represent about a 100,000 years. (Leading scholars currently tend to agree that *homo sapiens sapiens* is about this old, while several near relatives are much older.) In that case, the first instance of agriculture appeared in Western Asia a little after nine thirty in the evening. The first kind of writing, Sumeric cuneiform, was adopted in the same part of the world an hour later. Gutenberg's printing press saw the light of day at 8 minutes to midnight, and the conquest of America was begun by European soldiers and adventurers a few seconds later. The telephone and assembly line production are nearly a minute and a half old, while television and commercial air travel have existed for a mere 30 seconds. And the Internet? Forget it.

Seen from a perspective of cultural history, agriculture is a footnote, while modernity is a footnote under a footnote, if duration is all that counts. Hunters and gatherers, who *were* humanity for more than 90 per cent of our species history, have gradually been displaced to the most isolated and marginal parts of the world – the Arctic semi-desert, the Australian desert, the central African rainforest – and have been replaced by horticulturalists and agriculturalists with rapidly increasing population densities, before the phenomenal growth of industrial and informational society during the last couple of centuries.

The time gap between the great watersheds, or divides, in technological history has been progressively reduced. Writing had existed for 4,500 years before the printing press made books common. Printing had only only just cleared the table after the celebrations of its 500th anniversary when it was seriously challenged by electronic text, and the radio was only allowed its dominant position for a few decades before television turned it into a supplier of niche products. Similarly, it took 5,000 years from the introduction of the horse carriage until its replacement by combustion-engine powered automobiles with pneumatic tyres – a Roman time-traveller visiting Piccadilly Circus in 1890 would not have been shocked by innovations in urban transport technology – but the first aeroplane was invented only 20 years after the car.

The replacement of models and product variants today happens at such a speed that there scarcely exists a producer of anything at all who does not plan the next model before the latest model has been presented to the public. In theory, a product may eventually become obsolete before it reaches the shelves (in the world of computing, this actually happens every so often).

A description of the latest 10, 100, 200 or 10,000 years of cultural history that concentrates on acceleration, puts the finger on a central dimension of the humanly created part of the world. This perspective underlies the entire present analysis. Before moving to a consideration of acceleration and its effects, we shall nevertheless look into some of the main characteristics of our form of life, by which I simply mean modern society. Instead of entering into a complicated discussion about periodisation – when did modern society or modern culture begin? – I propose some simple contrasts between modern and non-modern societies. One is not exactly adored in academia for doing this, and for sound reasons: not only is modernity a notoriously difficult word which, among other things, has the side-effect of providing armies of academics with their daily bread – but, in their way, non-modern societies are just as different from each other as they are from ours. One is, in other words, faced with opposition from several academic camps when doing what I am about to do. As a defence plea, I will stress that the description that follows is correct at a general level, and that it indicates a clear direction in cultural history, from the concrete to the abstract. This is important, for the tyranny of the moment is the end-product of a long historical process that began when an unknown Sumerian genius discovered that a physical symbol could represent a spoken word. He or she liberated language from the speaker.

AFTER SPEECH AND VISUAL ART, WRITING MARKED A MAJOR WATERSHED IN INFORMATION TECHNOLOGY

Writing ranks high on anybody's list of the most important inventions in cultural history. Naturally, our kind of society would have been unthinkable without this technology. We would not even have been the same people.

Writing is a tool for the externalisation of thoughts, facts, assertions, emotions. It freezes them in approximately the same way as the museum freezes culture. In West Asian agricultural societies 4,000 to 5,000 years ago, writing was essentially used for two purposes: lists and religion. One made lists or inventories of inhabitants (in order to be able to tax them and enlist them in the army), sacks of grain, slaves and so on. The rulers thereby got a very different kind of overview over their empire than would have otherwise have been possible. Eventually, literacy was extended to include numeracy, and the Phoenicians' legendary gift for trade in the ancient Mediterranean world is ascribed to their adeptness at book-keeping.

The initial religious use of writing fell into two kinds: first, writing itself had a magical element, and incantations engraved into stone were thus used ritually. The literate were regarded as people endowed with almost supernatural powers, on a par with blacksmiths (today's newspaper incidentally features a web designer who has given himself the professional title 'technical wizard'). Second, writing could be used to record, freeze and thereby authorise particular versions of myths and moral principles. In this way, the foundation was laid for the modern religions, which are sometimes spoken of as 'religions of the Book', with their claim to verbatim authenticity, exact descriptions of creation, salvation, paradise and so on.

The technology of writing was developed in at least three, possibly four places independently: West Asia, Central America, China and (perhaps) Egypt. Apart from Chinese and related scripts, all scripts in the old world – from Arabic and Hebrew to the North Indian Devanagari syllabary and the Amharic script of Ethiopia – can probably be traced back to the Sumeric cuneiform. It was rudimentary, pictographic (one symbol represented one word), limited in its flexibility and could be difficult to learn. Eventually, this family of scripts was supplanted by alphabets – strictly speaking, the earliest were syllabaries, where a sign stood for a syllable; but eventually, scripts where a sign stood for a phoneme or sound became common.

However, the congruence between speech and writing is never perfect, although many who live in literate societies think so. Some scripts consist exclusively of consonants (the reader has to fill in the vowels personally), and most West European languages have more sounds than letters, even if accented letters are included. Writing is distinctive from speech, and written language influences spoken language.

The Phoenician alphabet is among the oldest, and it was imported and adapted by Greeks in the eighth century BC. At least one script had formerly been used to write Greek, namely, but it seems likely that they had been illiterate for centuries when they adopted the new alphabet. Known texts and fragments from the first period of the ancient Greek civilisation have clear traces of having been created in an intermediate period. Like the Mesopotamian epic *Gilgamesh* and the oldest books in the Bible, Homer's epics, for example, have elements of orality. They are based on stories that had been narrated for generations before being written down. With classical philosophy, from the sixth century BC onwards, it is different. In philosophers like Thales, Parmenides and Heraclitus, writing comes into its own for the first time as a transformer of thought. In mature Greek philosophy, particularly in Plato and Aristotle (fifth and fourth centuries BC), ideas are being formulated that would literally have been unthinkable without writing. Plato's dialogues and Aristotle's treatises consist of logically coherent, lengthy strings of reasoning, clear definitions and meta-discussions of the nature of language and words, all of which presupposes a clear distinction between a concept and its object. Language is, in other words, severed from the speech act, it is reified and externalised. The ideas can be subjected to critical examination, one may go back and forth in the text to check what the author said on the previous page, and one may examine, at one's leisure, the degree of logical coherence in the reasoning. The principles of logic, as they are presented and discussed in Aristotle's work, would have been difficult if not impossible to formulate in an oral culture. (However, as late as in Aristotle's time, there were still no standard conventions for punctuation and word spacing.)

The transition from mythical to philosophical thought is often described as 'the Greek Miracle'. In mythical thought, there is unity between speech act, linguistic concepts and external reality, while philosophy distinguishes between the three levels, and makes it possible to discuss the relationship between language and the world critically.

Writing made it possible to develop knowledge in a cumulative way, in the sense that one had access to, and could draw directly on, what others had done. One was no longer dependent on face-to-face contact with one's teachers. They had left their thoughts and discoveries for posterity in a material, frozen form. The quantitative growth in the total knowledge of humanity, to be dealt with in later chapters, is a result of writing. A Thomas Aquinas could, in the thirteenth century, spend an entire life trying to reconcile two important sets of texts – the Bible and Aristotle's philosophy – which were already then considered ancient. Explorers travelling in the Black Sea area in the sixth century AD could compare their observations with Herodotos' descriptions from the fifth century BC. Mathematicians and scientists could use Euclid and Archimedes as points of departure when setting out to develop new insights.

Writing makes it possible for us to stand firmly on the shoulders of deceased and remote ancestors, but it is also a pair of crutches for thought, which weakens the faculty of memory. When you can look it up, you no longer need to remember. Seen as a general principle, this insight seems to be a bad omen for the fate of the human spirit in information society.

A non-literate society has an oral religion where several versions of the most important myths usually circulate, where the extent of the religion is limited by the reach of the spoken word, and where there is no fixed set of dogmas that the faithful must adhere to. A literate society, on the contrary, usually has a written religion (often in the shape of sacred texts), with a theoretically unlimited geographic reach, with a clearly delineated set of dogmas and principles, and with authorised, 'correct' versions of myths and narratives. Such a religion can in principle be identical in the Arab peninsula and in Morocco (although it is never that simple in practice; local circumstances impinge on it, and oral traditions never die entirely). The three great religions of conversion from West Asia have all these characteristics, which they do not share with a single traditional African religion.

A non-literate society, further, has a judicial system based on custom and tradition, while a literate society has a legislative system. Morality in the non-literate society depends on interpersonal relations – it is embedded in tangible relationships between individuals – while morality in the literate society in theory is legalistic, that is, embedded in the written legislation. Even the relationship between parents and children is regulated by written law in our kind of society.

In a non-literate society, knowledge is transmitted from mouth to ear, and the people are forced to train their memory. The total reservoir of knowledge which is available at any particular point in time is embodied in those members of society that happen to be alive. When someone dies in a small, oral society, the net loss of knowledge can be considerable. (Later, I shall discuss the youth cult of the contemporary age in the context of accelerated change. One cause of the disdain of old age and the worship of youth is obviously the fact that our elders' knowledge is not lost when they die – only their wisdom, and that is a commodity with decreasing exchange-value in a fast-moving society.)

Most non-literate societies are organised on the basis of kinship, while literate societies tend to be state societies where an abstract ideology of community, such as nationalism, functions as a kind of metaphorical kinship. In certain non-state societies, religions of the Book have historically worked partly in the same way.

Observant readers will have noticed that I am simplifying to the extreme here, juxtaposing ancient Greek city-states and modern nation-states under the heading 'literate societies', and similarly talking in a vague fashion about 'non-literate societies'. This is correct, and for those who are interested in the details, there is an enormous professional literature about literacy and orality in a historical and comparative perspective. A great many societies can be located in the grey zone between literacy and orality: they represent hybrid forms. Some have used writing to a limited degree, while others have used it for purposes other than stimulating critical, scientific thought (religious indoctrination through rote learning of core texts, for example), and it is doubtless true that many European societies became fully literate only in the nineteenth century. These details, important as they are in research, are less relevant here; what matters in this context, is the general drift of history, and the point of this sketch is to offer a backdrop for an analysis of our own kind of society.

At a political level, the general tendency is that non-literate societies are either decentralised and egalitarian, or chiefdoms where political office is inherited. Literate societies, on the other hand, are strongly centralised, and tend to have a professional administration where office is in principle accorded following a formal set of rules.

In general, literate societies are much larger, both in geographic size and in population, than non-literate ones. And while the inhabitants of non-literate societies tell myths about who they are and where they come from, literate societies have *history* to perform the same functions, based on archives and other written sources.

It should be clear by now that writing has been an essential tool in the transition from what we could call a *concrete society* based on intimate, personal relationships, memory, local religion and orally transmitted myths, to an *abstract society* based on formal legislation, archives, a book religion and written history. I shall mention four other technological innovations which, together with writing, indicate those peculiar characteristics of modern society that are preconditions for information society.

THE CLOCK WAS INTRODUCED TO REGULATE PRAYER TIMES; WHAT DOES IT REGULATE NOW?

The clock was developed in the European medieval age, probably to synchronise prayer times in the monasteries. (The calls of the Muslim *muezzin* and the Christian church bells are contemporary reminders of this initial function of timing technology.) Calendars are older, and were developed independently in many more places than writing. In general, however, calendars in non-modern societies were not a technical aid to help societies make five-year plans and individuals to keep track of their daily schedules and deadlines, but were rather linked with the seasons, ritual cycles, astronomy and the agricultural year. The clock is more accurate and more minute (literally) than the calendar. It measures time as well as cutting it into quantifiable segments. In spite of its initially religious function, the clock rapidly spread to coordinate other fields of activity as well. The Dutch thinker Hugo Grotius (1583–1645) formulated a moral maxim which illustrates this. Grotius is widely known for his contributions to political philosophy, but he is also sometimes mentioned as the first modern European to defend a moral principle completely divorced from religion: 'Punctuality is a virtue!' ('Time is money' is a later refinement of this principle, usually attributed to Benjamin Franklin.)

In the same way as writing externalises language, clocks externalise time. Time becomes 'something' existing independently of human experience, something objective and measurable. This was definitely not the case in traditional societies, where inhabitants lived within an event-driven time structure in their everyday existence. Events regulate the passage of time, not the other way around. If a traveller, or an ethnographer, to an African village wonders when a certain event will take place, the answer may be: 'When everything is ready.' Not, in other words, 'at a quarter to five'. But today, there are no clear-cut distinctions. Even in societies where clocks and time-tables have made their entry long ago, it may well be that they are not directly connected to people's everyday life. A colleague who conducted fieldwork in the Javanese countryside reports that one day, he needed to take a train to the nearest town. So he asked a man when the train was due. The man looked at him with the proverbial puzzled expression, and pointed to the tracks: 'The train comes from that direction, then it stops here, and after a little while it continues in the other direction.'

Clock time turns time into an autonomous entity, something that exists independently of events. 'An hour' may exist (in our minds) in an abstract way; it is an empty entity that can be filled with anything. Hence it is common to speak of clock time as 'empty, quantified time'. It is chopped up into accurately measured 'pieces', like metres and decilitres. These entities are presupposed to be identical for everybody, anywhere and any time. Living in our kind of society entails that each of us signs a contract the moment we are born, committing us to lifelong faith in clock-and-calendar time. (The contract sometimes takes a while to become operative. My son, who is 3, thus often insists that it is Sunday and time for TV cartoons and a day of anarchic mayhem at home with his little sister, even if the calendar indicates that it is Tuesday and time for kindergarten.)

In the present context, two aspects of clock time are particularly important: First, it turns time into an exact, objective and abstract entity, a straitjacket for the flows and ebbs of experienced time perhaps – for this kind of time will always pass at varying speed; as everybody knows, 5 minutes can be anything from a moment to an eternity. The philosopher who has developed the most systematic assault on this quantitative time tyranny, is doubtless Henri Bergson (1859–1941). He was perhaps the most famous intellectual in the world in the interwar years, and received the Nobel Prize for literature in 1928. In his doctoral treatise from 1889, *Sur les données immédiates de la conscience* ('On the immediate givens of consciousness'), rendered in English as *Time and Free Will*, he severely criticises the quantitative, 'empty' time that regulates us from the outside, instead of letting the tasks at hand fill the time from within.

Second, the clock synchronises everybody who has been brought within its charmed circle. Everyone who reads this is in agreement regarding what it means when we say that it is, say, 8.15 p.m. Everybody knows when to turn on the television to watch a particular programme, and they do it simultaneously, independently of each other. If the programme has already begun when one turns it on, it is not because the TV channel has failed to meet its commitments, but because something is wrong with the viewer's timepiece. (Television is a very strongly synchronising kind of technology and has played a major role in nation-building in the latter half of the twentieth century; interestingly, when the move is made from single-channel to multi-channel television, it seems to work in exactly the opposite way. More about this later.) Coordination of complex production in factories and office environments would also, naturally, have been unthinkable without the clock, as would anything from public transport to cinema shows.

The thermometer does the same to temperature as the clock does to time. Under thermometer-driven regimes, it is not acceptable to state merely that it 'feels cold' when one can walk over to the thermometer and obtain the exact number of degrees. If it shows more than 20 degrees Celsius, it is not the air temperature, as it were, but oneself that is to be blamed.

MONEY BELONGS TO THE SAME FAMILY OF INFORMATION
TECHNOLOGIES AS WRITING AND CLOCKS

A more consequential kind of technology than the thermometer is another invention which pulls adherents and victims in the same direction, namely money. In traditional societies, both language and time concepts exist, but not writing and clocks. Similarly, money-like instruments exist in many kinds of societies, but our kind of money, 'general-purpose money', is recent and historically culture-bound. It does roughly the same thing to payment, value measurements and exchange as clocks and writing do to time and language, respectively. They make the transaction abstract and impose a standardised grid on to a large area (ultimately the whole world). They place individual, mundane transactions under an invisible umbrella of abstraction.

Shell money, gold coins and other compact valuables are known from a wide range of traditional societies. They may, perhaps, be used as value standards to make different goods comparable – a bag of grain equals half a gold coin; a goat equals half a gold coin; *ergo*, a sack of grain can be bartered with a goat. They may be used as means of exchange; I can buy two goats with a gold coin. They may even be used as means of payment – I have killed my neighbour, and have to pay the widow and children three gold coins in compensation. However, modern money is a much more powerful technology than anything comparable that we know from traditional societies. Above all, it is *universal* in its field of applicability. It may be that Lennon and McCartney were correct in their view that love is not a marketable commodity (although it is easy to find cynical sociologists who argue to the contrary), but in general, one single kind of money functions as a universal means of payment and exchange, and as a value standard. West African cowries had no value outside a limited area, and, even there, only certain commodities and services could be purchased with them. General-purpose money is legal tender in an entire state of millions of inhabitants, and if we belong to a country with a convertible currency, it is valid worldwide. Regarded as information technology, money has truly contributed to the creation of one world, albeit a world into which only people of means are integrated. Money makes wages and purchasing-power all over the world comparable, makes it possible to exchange a tonne of taro from New Guinea with electronics from Taiwan, and it is a necessary medium for the world economy to be possible at all. Whereas transaction and trade in many societies depended on trust and personal relationships between seller and buyer, the abstract and universal money we are familiar with, implies an externalisation of economic transactions. As long as there is agreement over the economic value of the coloured bits of paper, I need not know either my debtors or my creditors. With the recent move of money into cyberspace, which entails that the same plastic card can be used for economic transactions nearly anywhere in the world, it becomes even more abstract.

NOTATION DOES THE SAME KIND OF WORK AS WRITING, NUMBERS, CLOCKS AND MONEY

My last example for now is musical notation. Most (all?) societies we know possess some kind of music, but notation was only invented a couple of times, namely in Europe (ninth century AD) and China/Japan (tenth century AD). However, it was only in Europe that an expressed aim of notation from the very beginning was to create an entirely symbolic language for communicating musical content – the Chinese/Japanese system was based on pictographs proper to the written language. In the beginning, the rudimentary notes marked only ascent and descent of tone level. Eventually, they became more accurate, and in the eleventh century, Guido of Arezzo introduced the staff, which made it possible to mark specified intervals. In the same period, the notation system was standardised, and symbolic markers depicting tone duration were also introduced. At the beginning of the sixteenth century, the system with which we are familiar was largely in place.

Several aspects of musical notation are relevant in the present context. First, notes do the same to music as script does to language; they liberate music from the performer, and make it possible to store music independently of people as well as for individual players to learn a piece without personal contact with another performer. Only those aspects of music that can be depicted in writing are transmitted. Just as there is an indefinite residue in speech that is not transmitted through texts, the same could be said of music (feeling and, for a long time, pitch and speed, are three such aspects). Second, notes freeze music, just as history freezes myths and clock time fixes the variable flow of time. In several European countries, folk music that had evolved gradually for centuries, was suddenly transcribed and preserved in frozen form during national romanticism; as a result, it is played today note by note as it was played, say, in the mid-nineteenth century. Third, notation lays the conditions for another kind of complexity than would otherwise have been possible. Tellingly, notation was developed in the same period as polyphony, a musical innovation which appeared only in Europe. Neither the mathematical regularity of Bach's fugues nor the very large number of voices in Beethoven's symphonies would have been possible without an accurate system of notation. The standard tone A440 (a pure A is a wave with the frequency 440) was finally defined in 1939, after having fluctuated for hundreds of years. It is the equivalent in music to the gold standard, Greenwich Mean Time and the meter rod in Paris. A shared, abstract standard is assumed to be valid for all persons at all times.

SOCIETY BECOMES INCREASINGLY ABSTRACT

The spread of the technology of writing led to the standardisation of languages. The technology of the clock led to both the standardisation of time units and the synchronisation of large populations. The larger the number of people who needed to coordinate their movements with minute precision, the larger were the regions that were comprised by the new standards. When the last stretch of the Great Western Railway was opened in June 1841, the clocks in Bristol ran 10 minutes behind clocks in London. There had been no need for an exact synchronisation of the inhabitants of the two cities until then. This need for synchronisation came partly with the railway, partly with the telegraph during the following decades. The railway reduced the 20-hour journey from London to Bristol to 4 hours, but the telegraph soon reduced the time required to send urgent despatches almost to zero.

The present global system of 24 time zones was established in 1884. A maze of local time zones had made conversion difficult earlier, and the need for a common standard had been voiced for years when an international panel finally reached an agreement at a meeting in Washington, DC.

The transitions from kinship to national identity, from custom to legislation, from 'cowrie money' or similar to general-purpose money, from internalised music to notation, from local religions to written religions of conversion, from person-dependent morality to universalistic morality, from memory to archives, from myths to history, and from event-driven time to clock time, all point in the same direction: from a small-scale society based on concrete social relations and practical knowledge to a large-scale society based on an abstract legislative system and abstract knowledge founded in logic and science.

This kind of contrast has been popular in the social and historical sciences, but it has gone out of fashion. Most scholars are presently more preoccupied with explorations of the particularities of single societies than with gross generalisations. And naturally, with very sound reasons. In reality, traditional forms of knowledge exist side by side with the modern ones. Nepotism, anachronistic religious notions and faith in unspecified 'spirits' (never walk under a ladder, do not open an umbrella indoors), intuition and spontaneous creativity continue to exist in modern as well as traditional societies, as do kinship and person-dependent moralities. In my own work, I have written a short book about the parallels between myth and history, and much of my academic research has dealt with a modern phenomenon which shares many features with kinship, namely ethnicity. So the objection to these grand generalisations is valid, but only if one insists on using a magnifying glass. I remain confident that the dimensions that have been identified do demarcate major differences between life on Manhattan and life in a remote Melanesian village.

Two further historical changes, with important implications for both thought and way of life, need mentioning at the end: printing and the Industrial Revolution.

Before the era of print – Gutenberg lived from about 1400 to 1468 – literacy existed in many societies, but it was not particularly widespread. There were several causes for this; among other things, the fact that a book could be as costly as a small farm. Books were always written by hand, largely by monks, but also by professional copyists. Then Gutenberg invented his printing press – frequently seen as the single most important invention of the last 2,000 years – and suddenly, books became inexpensive, from 1455 and onwards, to be exact (this was the year Gutenberg printed the famous 42-line Bible). Books did not become really cheap immediately. Gutenberg's Bible cost 30 guilders, and the annual salary for a worker was 10 guilders. During the following decades, the new technology spread to cover the central parts of Europe, and books became increasingly inexpensive. The first printing shop in England was founded by William Caxton in 1476. Caxton was printer, editor, book salesman and publisher (a common combination as late as the nineteenth century), and he contributed in no small degree to standardising English orthography and syntax. Printing entailed standardisation in other countries as well, and facilitated access to books written in native languages, at the expense of Latin. The market was suddenly much larger than the small elite of Latin scholars. Printing was a decisive factor for the emergence of new science, philosophy and literature in early modern times. It was crucial for both mass education and the creation of civil society in European cities, and led to consequences Gutenberg could never have foreseen. His main ambitions seem to have been to print Bibles and pay his debts.

The features of printing that are most relevant here, are its contribution to the spectacular growth in information, and its standardising aspect. Cheap, printed books contributed to the standardisation of both language and world-views. An identical message, clothed in identical linguistic garb, could now be broadcast to the entire middle class from Augsburg to Bremen. Thus a national public sphere could emerge for the first time, consisting of equals who were preoccupied with the same writers, the same political and theological questions, the same philosophical, geographic and scientific novelties. Printing was so important for the development of democracy and nationalism that Benedict Anderson gave the leading role to print capitalism in his historical drama about the rise of nationalism, *Imagined Communities*. Without this formidable system of production and distribution, it is difficult to see how a person in Marseilles could even dream of having a morally committing feeling of community with a person in Lille. Seen as a technological device for creating abstract communities, that is solidarity and empathy between people who will never meet in the flesh, print capitalism is king. The underlying question for us is, naturally: if print capitalism bequeathed nationalism and democracy, what lies in store for us after a period similarly dominated by the Internet and digital satellite television?

It took a long time for literacy to become truly widespread even after the rise of printing technology. In Shakespeare's time, perhaps 10 per cent of the population in England and Wales were literate. No country has an illiteracy rate even approaching this today. Even women in conservative, patriarchal societies have a higher literacy rate than the citizens of Shakespeare's England.

It was printing coupled with universal primary education and mass media like newspapers and magazines (including books published in monthly instalments) that truly pulled the minds of ordinary men and women into the new, abstract society. This society consisted of an enormous number of persons who were all cogs in a giant machine, and eventually they could easily be replaced by others in the productive process. Their knowledge and skills were not unique, but standardised and therefore comparable to others' knowledge and skills. With the Industrial Revolution in the nineteenth century, this possibility was turned into practice for the first time.

While traditional crafts were transferred directly from master to apprentice, production in a factory is so standardised that, ideally, it only requires a few, general skills. (The same thing may with some justice be said about the 'production' of a bureaucracy; whether one has graduated from Durham or Sussex makes little difference.) The early sociologists, from Marx to Durkheim, were concerned with factory production, which entails splitting up the process so that each worker only produces a tiny bit of the whole. Criticisms to the effect that this led to alienation were made not just by Marx, but by a lot of concerned observers in the nineteenth century, that is, a generation or two before Henry Ford invented the conveyor belt. Things would, in other words, only get worse. Or perhaps better: Like books, manufactured goods became cheaper and more easily available.

Industrial production synchronises work and standardises its products. An item, such as, say, a mini-disc recorder, is identical with all other items of the same make and model, and if it is unique, that is because of some defect. In the society of craftmanship, on the contrary, each object was individually made and unique.

The time recorder and the factory clock belong to the industrial mode of production. Thus the chronometer had finally gone the whole way, from the pastoral communities of monasteries to large-scale industrial society.

Modern societies are characterised by a particular kind of complexity. It is not the only one possible. Indian caste society and traditional Australian world-views are two spectacular examples of social and cultural complexity, respectively. Nonetheless, modernity was, in the latter half of the twentieth century, in a uniquely important position; it was hegemonic on the verge of becoming universal. It synchronises and standardises an enormous number of persons, all of them little cogs in a great machinery. It draws on a shared mechanical time-structure, a global medium for economic transactions (money), a technology of production and destruction based on a shared theoretical science. Modernity coordinates the movements and thoughts of an enormous number of people in ways which are both unknown and unthinkable in non-modern societies. It makes particular individuals superfluous by externalising time, language, economy, memory, morality and knowledge. And it lays the foundation for a nearly infinite social complexity. Forever new millions of people can be drawn into the system through its simple common denominators, without it changing character or needing reorganisation.

LINEAR TIME IS NOT PART OF THE PROBLEM

Still I have not even mentioned *the faith in progress*. To some, this is the very quintessence of modernity, and some – both pessimists and optimists – believe that we have initiated a truly postmodern era since the universal faith in progress seems to be disappearing. The idea that historical change moves in a particular direction is important in the legitimation of modern societies. Knowledge, techniques, morality, standards of living, knowledge – all of this, it has been assumed, progresses. The electronic gadgets of today are better than yesterday's gadgets, the philosophers of the twentieth century understood more than those working in the eighteenth century, and, all things taken into account, humanity is more at ease with itself today than in earlier periods. If this last assumption should not, after all, prove correct, the proper antidote has been even more faith in progress, possibly of a competing brand (such as socialism).

Linear time is an important dimension of the faith in progress, and as will later be shown, its failure is a key factor in creating the tyranny of the moment. Now, linear time is not a necessary consequence of clocks and calendars. The clock actually records temporal cycles lasting for 12 or 24 hours. As the readers will recall, the tired joke about defective clocks notes that they are not entirely worthless: they are correct twice a day. Calendars with numbered years and days, on the contrary, point forward, but most of the traditional calendars we know – from Thailand to Central America – have referred to cyclical ritual epochs, not to historical change. It is the clock plus printing plus science and engineering plus industrial production plus capitalism that constitutes the cultural package which creates the faith in progress. It is a powerful package. And yet, many of us have an unpleasant feeling that something is about to go terribly wrong; that the world is not necessarily becoming a better, more just, humane and manageable place, or at least that events do not necessarily point in any particular direction. This feeling is not caused by linear time, but by a time perception which is no longer sufficiently linear. There are limits as to how many pieces one can partition time into before it ceases to exist as duration, and the only time in existence is a single, manic, hysterical moment which is continuously changed, but which does not point any further into the future than to the next moment. Ironically, the forces that led to the development of linear time and the faith in progress may, at a particular stage in their development, lead to the exact opposite.

Perhaps the problem that is taken on in this book is ultimately caused by the fact that modern societies were too successful in their attempts to make everybody more efficient, to achieve more, to streamline, standardise and accelerate their immanent process of change. Change, or 'progress', now takes place so fast that it has become impossible to relate to it sensibly. And when something happens all the time, nothing really happens. Speed is a key factor in bringing this paradoxical situation about, and to that we now turn.

4 Speed

Everything moves so fast
these days. Not just time,
not just the plane
to America,
cars, trains and ships,
not just music.

The Japanese
have reduced the time to four minutes and fifteen seconds
in a recording of Beethoven's fifth
symphony. That's how fast things are.

The above is quoted from the popular Norwegian poet and performer Odd Börretzen. His mention of a certain Japanese orchestra is witty, but sometimes satire pales by comparison with reality. An ageing diva at Oslo's national theatre thus recalls a performance of Ibsen's *Rosmersholm* which lasted a full 4 hours. The most recent staging of the play, from 1998, lasted for 1 hour and 58 minutes. There were no major cuts or deletions in the dialogue.

It is curious that Börretzen should mention Beethoven; so does Milan Kundera, in his beautiful little novel *La Lenteur* (*Slowness*) from 1995. There is a scene where a key character in Kundera's story, a Czech scientist, sits in a hotel room, reflecting over the sheer speed in news broadcasts, mulling over how fragments give way to new fragments without any particular order, without an overarching narrative; how it has become patently impossible to weave those snippets of news that flash by into that large tapestry called History, and how every flash is presented in a breathless and impatient way because the next flash is already eager and waiting in the wings. Contemporary history, he says, is narrated in the same way as a concert where the orchestra plays all of Beethoven's 138 works consecutively, but only the first eight bars of each. In another 10 years, he reflects, they will only play the first note of each piece – 138 notes altogether. 'And in twenty years, the whole of Beethoven's music would be summed up in a single very long buzzing tone, like the endless sound he heard the first day of his deafness.'

Kundera and Börretzen are right. Everything seems to move faster and faster. As I sat by my desk in relative peace and quiet one morning in May 2000, jotting down notes and fragments for this book, I was interrupted by three simultaneous and identical e-mails marked with red tags ('Priority: High!'), followed by a physical visit from the secretary, who actually walked around in the corridor, knocking on doors and warning the inhabitants of imminent danger. Since we got e-mail, we hardly see our secretary any more, and so we immediately understood that the situation had to be very serious.

Now, the reason for this unusual and dramatic behaviour was neither a fire on the first floor, a general strike, an attempted *coup d'état* by the military or even an escalating and spontaneous wave of suicides among university employees protesting against the decay of our institution, but a small computer program that had infected many of our hard disks. A virus! The virus program had arrived as an attachment to an e-mail entitled 'ILOVEYOU', which contained a plea for the recipient to open the attached 'love letter from me to you'. If one did – and many did, understandably, given that they had been promised an unconditional declaration of love – a malign virus would begin deleting files, messing up data and then proceed to move on to other innocent computers via the victim's electronic address list. A surprising number of colleagues received the virus before lunch on that day, generally from different sources, and many got it twice or even three times.

The virus, which in a matter of hours had been nicknamed 'The Love Worm', was first observed in Hong Kong late in the evening on Wednesday, 3 May (local time). When the population of the USA got out of bed a little while later (and it was Wednesday morning in the US), the virus began to move across the world with astonishing speed. Within the next couple of days it had reached – among many other places – the University of Gothenburg, a weekly Oslo newspaper and the Norwegian Institute of International Studies, and arrived from individual computers in all three places at my computer on Thursday morning. As people began to return home from work on that fateful Thursday, the leading anti-virus companies had already developed remedies which were freely available on the web. The virus was virulent and epidemic from the very beginning (other viruses, such as that which carries bubonic plague, may be passive for years before turning vicious), and the entire epidemic lasted less than three days. Within that span, between 60 per cent and 80 per cent of the computers in the USA were estimated to have been infected to a greater or lesser degree. On Thursday evening, CNN online reported that the Scandinavian photo agency Scanpix had lost 4,500 images, in spite of impeccable security routines.

A couple of days' epidemic dissemination all over the world were brought to an abrupt end, following the spread of prominent warnings in virtually all the world's media. A week later, the virus makers were arrested by the Filipino police.

One cannot help comparing this epidemic with earlier major epidemics in European history. The most famous and, possibly, the most consequential was the Black Death (1347–51). It had already caused mass death and political fragmentation in large parts of Europe for a couple of years when it finally reached Bergen in 1349, arriving in the Baltic lands only the next year. It took the plague three years to make the trip from Sicily to Riga, in spite of the fact that it was extremely contagious. Excepting the immediate neighbouring areas (West Asia and North Africa), no other continents than Europe were affected. Indeed, the great plague of the 530s was more global – it started in East Africa and caused havoc in China, Arabia and Europe – and it moved just as fast as the plague 800 years later. Whatever was far away in space, in the fourteenth as well as in the sixth century, was also far removed in time.

OUR HISTORY IS THE HISTORY OF ACCELERATION

There are many possible theoretical approaches to our near past, and the history of modernity has kept generations of academics and students busy for more than a century. Some concentrate on the history of ideas, while others emphasise economics or politics. It can be done differently. For example, it can be highly illuminating to view the history of the last 200 years as a history of acceleration. Strangely, this dimension is rarely foregrounded in the extensive literature on globalisation. The reason why this is surprising is simply that globalisation is itself tantamount to a particular form of acceleration, which reduces the importance of distance, frequently obliterating it altogether. In the era of wireless communications, there is no longer a connection between duration and distance. As the theorist of speed, Paul Virilio, puts it: we now live in an era with no delays.

Virilio had the Internet family of technologies in mind, and thus he was not overstating the point. As the reader realises, he was thinking neither of commuter trains nor of citizens waiting to speak to a bureaucrat on the phone. Global telecommunications and other communication based on satellites are placeless and immediate. All the nodes connected through the Net are in reality both in the same place, everywhere and nowhere. In practice, there is no difference between sending and receiving e-mail from Melbourne or from the office next door; or watching a direct transmission from a football game in Belgium, New Year celebrations in Kiribati or an interview transmitted from one's local television studio. Time, regarded as a means to create distance and proximity, is gone.

This familiar fact has many unintended consequences, some of which are explored by Virilio, who talks of his own field of study as *dromology*, the study of speed and acceleration. One of his special fields of interest is the military. A century ago, it would take weeks or months to invade a country like Poland: the speed of war was identical with the average speed of the cavalry. Although horses are fast animals, they need food and rest, and they are further delayed by hills, swamps and rivers – not to mention intransigent villagers who destroy bridges and set traps. At the beginning of the last century, the tank and the double-decker airplane were introduced, and suddenly the speed of war was greatly increased. Then came the Spitfires and medium-range missiles, and, today, a warlike state can in principle inflict unspeakable damage on another country in a matter of minutes.

One of Virilio's sources of inspiration is the media theorist Marshall McLuhan, perhaps most widely known for his optimistic slogan 'the global village' where all of humanity participates in a magnificent conversation about values, beauty and its own shared destiny. Virilio prefers to speak of a 'global mega-city' characterised by anonymity and disintegration, where everybody communicates with everybody else, and where nobody – for that very reason – really speaks with anyone. This 'virtual city' is organised by means of real-time information technology. In other words, we have a situation where time dominates space. Distances vanish, and when that which is far away becomes as close as that which is near, nothing is really near any more, according to Virilio.

Virilio's pessimism is close kin to that of the classic sociology of the latter half of the nineteenth century; authors like Ferdinand Tönnies and Georg Simmel wrote in a worried (Tönnies) or fascinated (Simmel) mode about the anonymity of urban life, about individualism and the loss of authority in tradition and religion, and about that pragmatic, goal-oriented style of behaviour that is so typical of industrial society. Does this mean that the problems raised by acceleration are older than we seem to think? The answer is, as usual when one raises unanswerable questions, yes and no.

Every generation has a tendency to regard its own era as being unique, and with good reason: all epochs are in their way unique. At the same time, it can also be claimed that much of that which is perceived as novel, has in fact existed for quite a while – say, since Plato, or since the agricultural revolution, since Marco Polo, Columbus, Gutenberg or the Reformation (take your pick). Regarding speed and acceleration, one may object, to those who stress the unique aspects of jet planes and the Internet, that the most important changes took place when the telegraph was invented, or the steamship, or for that matter the fast Roman two-wheel chariot. In other words, there is little or nothing new under the sun.

This kind of argument has its limitations. Although the telegraph was an invention with enormous consequences, the Internet signifies more than a mere footnote to Marconi. Global telecommunications based on real time create a framework for human existence which differs radically from that of all earlier technologies. Yet it is correct to regard the electronic revolution as a direct extension of earlier innovations and accelerations. The previous chapter discussed the implications of some great informational divides in Western cultural history – writing, money, printing, the clock. All these contributed to liberating, as it were, communication from its immediate context; writing made knowledge timeless and cumulative, the clock made time mechanical and universal; money made values comparable. Whether one is in Canberra or in Kanpur, a dollar, an hour and a news headline mean pretty much the same. The circumstances continue to vary, but the common denominators link places together.

Standardisation and time-saving are true-born children of the Industrial Revolution, and it was during the disruptions caused by industrialisation that the foundations for the tyranny of the moment were laid. Only in industrial society could the clock be used to promote synchronised efficiency in a large and complex industrial work setting. It was also in this era that time and money were tightly coupled; punctuality had been a virtue at least since the time of Erasmus, but the notion that time saved is money made became a guiding principle in production only when industry replaced traditional crafts on a large scale. The Industrial Revolution, which began towards the end of the eighteenth century, would need the entire nineteenth century to be completed in the West, culminating in the introduction of assembly lines and time recorders.

Living in this era of acceleration and fast change, the general public was partly fascinated, partly frightened. New kinds of commodities were produced in frightful quantities; the colonial empires expanded and created a world economy based – like today's world economy – largely on exports of raw materials from the poor countries and exports of manufactured goods from the rich countries. Trains, steamships, telegraph and telephone lines all contributed in no small measure to the shrinking of the world in ways that must have seemed no less impressive than the current shrinking process. During the nineteenth century, fashion in clothing began to change at a new pace, and the notion of 'this year's Paris models' appeared.

The inhabitants of Europe and North America were concerned with the effects of speed, the shrinking of distance and what we would today call globalisation, as they are today (and, like today, they were generally more enthusiastic on the western coast of the Atlantic than on the eastern coast). In 1824, the steam railway was a recent invention, and some foresighted commentators immediately realised that it would change the world. 'When the steam carriage becomes widespread, it is not particularly daring to predict that the present extreme speed [10 miles an hour] may be doubled', wrote a journalist in *The Scotsman*. He further notes that the Americans, 'with their characteristic eye for improvements', had begun to study this brand-new technology, and envision a future where even the wondrous speed of 20 miles an hour might be doubled. Interestingly, the Scottish commentator draws comparisons of the same kind as those commonly used today when a new, accelerating technology is introduced: he states that 'the tour of Europe' (which then included Paris and Florence), soon could be undertaken in the same time as 'our grandfathers' had needed to travel from Edinburgh to London.

In spite of ever faster trains and attempts to compete with air traffic, European railway companies nowadays try to position themselves as offering a contemplative, quiet alternative to the hectic bustle of air travelling and the frustrations of driving. Travelling by train, one may enjoy *slow time*. This concept of the train – as a romantic vestige of a bygone era (a form of nostalgia which is particularly well developed in Britain, the home of trainspotters and Thomas the Tank Engine) – is very far removed from its original significance. Turner's painting *Rain, Steam and Speed* from 1844 brings out the spirit of the age in this respect. It depicts the Great Western Railway as the train crosses a bridge just west of London. The picture suggests an almost unreal speed, a movement so quick that the human eye has difficulty perceiving it. The train moved at an average velocity of 20 miles an hour, although it could in theory reach all of 50 miles an hour on certain stretches. When the first railway in Norway, from Christiania (Oslo) to Eidsvold some 60 kilometres to the north, was opened in 1855, the average speed was less than 20 miles an hour, and yet many were worried. They felt that the unnaturally high speed of the steam train made it difficult to take in the details of the landscape when one was travelling. It challenged the natural boundaries of human perception, it was said.

Literally in parallel with the steam railway, telegraph lines mushroomed – they were often built along the railway tracks. This invention, which has been described as the Internet of the Victorian age, perhaps represented the most important change in the history of information technology since Gutenberg. For the first time, messages were severed from physical objects. For the first time, despatches could be sent for many miles in packets with a weight of less than 1 gram. The germ of the WWW was, in other words, sown in 1838. The network of telegraph lines grew extremely rapidly by the standards of the mid-nineteenth century, and the first trans-atlantic cable was operative already in 1866. This really represented something new. Only a few decades earlier, communication between Europe and the USA had taken weeks or months, depending on the season and weather conditions. Then, towards the end of the 1830s, steamships made sailships obsolete, and less than 30 years later, one could cable messages from London to New York. When the wireless telegraph was launched, just before the last turn of the century, it could indeed be said that mere cosmetics (or, actually, electronics) remained before the Internet was a reality. It was no longer necessary for millions of European migrants to wait for weeks and months to hear the latest news about their ageing relatives. They would receive a cable on the same day that their ailing uncle finally expired. In 1876, Bell patented the telephone, and it became common within a few decades, although one would have to wait until 1927 for the first functioning transatlantic lines. To all this, it must be added that global trade grew enormously in the latter half of the nineteenth century (another parallel to the 1990s), and the British Empire – then a powerhouse of technological change – became known as the colonial empire where the sun never set. The idea of a tightly integrated global society was, understandably, as widespread in the 1890s as it was in the 1990s, and was generally perceived in a more optimistic way.

The big cities grew, the selection of goods grew, tourism became a mass phenomenon, weekly magazines were established and became popular among all classes, and the newspapers competed ferociously for the latest news: the new society that was established in the late nineteenth century in the richest countries, with Great Britain, France and the United States at the forefront, had a lot in common with the society we live in today. It was characterised by acceleration, growing complexity, a sense of uprootedness and fast technological change. The very icon of global modernity in the twentieth century – Coca-Cola – was launched in 1886, and early advertisements promised that it countered 'slowness of thought'. It is true that the cocaine was taken out of the secret recipe in 1905, but millions of contemporary devotees would still agree that what Coca-Cola does for them is precisely to counteract slowness, if not necessarily of thought.

A key person in the transformation of work that took place about 100 years ago, was the American engineer Frederick W. Taylor (1856–1915). He was not the first to use time studies to monitor workers, but he developed a method which would almost immediately leave its deep mark on the industrial world. In Taylor's view, it was always or nearly always possible to make production more efficient by measuring the duration of every act the workers did, and then to eliminate the 'wastage' – not just the breaks, but also unnecessary bodily movements. His method, admired and detested under the name *Taylorism*, made it possible, almost as a side-effect, to chop up the productive process into a great number of constituent parts, and thus cleared the ground for assembly line production, where every single worker performs a small number of mechanical, repeated movements. Taylorism is, in a way, the response of industrial society to the metric system of measurement: it standardises, chops up and eradicates subjectivity.

The noisy, fast and anonymous life characterising the productive process, communication technology and – increasingly – the consumption of the second half of the nineteenth century, was perceived as something new. Not everybody was equally impressed.

The novelist Knut Hamsun, who lived and worked in the USA for several years in the 1880s, was at the outset impressed by the great technical advances of the country. In a letter to a friend, he described the enormous Brooklyn Bridge, all steel joints and huge bolts, in lyrical terms; and he also included a curious description of an early lift, which he describes as 'a seesaw-like device' (*et slags Vippeindretning*). When, in 1889, he wrote his essay 'On the Spiritual Life of Modern America', he had changed his mind. He now poked fun at the American tendency to embrace uncritically anything new, their disdain for tradition and their energetic and – in his view – quite unjustified optimism and naïve faith in progress. 'And the Americans themselves are convinced that all this restlessness and energy and rapid turning-around is a trait that freedom itself has ingrained into the American national character.'

In describing the 'typically American' attitude to change in these terms, Hamsun both echoes Alexis de Tocqueville (who wrote his influential work on America half a century earlier), anticipates contemporary European critics of the 'dot com' era, and closely parallels Rudyard Kipling. The young Kipling's first visit to America was much shorter than Hamsun's, but he returned with many of the same views on the perils of letting oneself be sucked up by a technological environment where speed rules with few or no countervailing forces. Kipling, whose essay aroused furious reactions in the US when it was published, was particularly concerned with what he saw as the vulgarisation and simplification of the English language (reminding one of another late Victorian luminary, namely Oscar Wilde, who once wrote of Americans that they and Britons had so much in common, except, of course, language). Linguistic simplification can, of course, be seen as a kind of acceleration – the art of speaking economically.

Acceleration in the nineteenth century was caused by the Industrial Revolution and new productivity demands in commodity production, aided by information technology. In the acceleration of the twenty-first century, information technology is simultaneously catalyst, source of coveted goods and economic powerhouse. That hurried, fragmented kind of existence which leads to so many frustrations and time traps nowadays is, to a certain extent, old news, satirically depicted by Hamsun, Kipling and others more than 100 years ago; but the information society also adds some genuinely new features to the situation. Speed is modern, and modernity has existed for at least a couple of hundred years. The principles of speed that I shall formulate later in this book are phrased in general ways, but they are only relevant in modern societies. Furthermore, the examples will indicate that there are indeed aspects of this particular phase in modernity – the post-Cold War period, the information age – which are unique.

SPEED IS AN ADDICTIVE DRUG

The topic has not properly reached the agenda of the 2000s yet, but it is about time that it did. The acceleration that was observed, commented upon and occasionally criticised by people of the nineteenth century has continued to this day, and it became more acutely felt than ever as computer networks and satellite-based communication linked the world more closely together than any telegraph or steamship company could even contemplate doing.

A long, long time ago, all letters were written by hand, and they were distributed through slow mail services (horse and carriage, sailing ships, etc.). Writing a letter took a long time, and distributing it took even longer. In the course of the nineteenth century, it wasn't just the production and distribution of letters that were accelerated: the typewriter appeared, a few decades after trains and steamships had made distribution safer and swifter. A few decades into the twentieth century, aeroplanes also began to be used in the distribution of mail. Now, it was suddenly possible to keep in touch with one's beloved in Australia and America without having to wait for months for them to respond. In the 1950s, abandoned relatives in Europe might even get a return letter from Minnesota in a mere three weeks, with a bit of luck.

And now? Nowadays we start to wait impatiently for the reply about 30 seconds after pressing the 'Send' button on the screen.

This form of acceleration has several kinds of consequences, not to say side-effects. The advantage, and purpose, inherent in e-mail is that it facilitates the act of contacting others. In comparison with the telephone, it is also said that it is more tactful, since sending an e-mail does not interrupt and divert people from whatever it is that they are doing. On the other hand, by the very same token, e-mail precludes absence: one can always be reached; one is never simply out to lunch.

In the old days, when we were still using dead trees for most of our correspondence, there was an inbuilt inertia in the material base of the information technology that inhibited untimely pestering.

Put differently, the technology itself offered resistance which made the work of writing a letter sufficiently laborious to filter out many unnecessary letters. The writing itself took time, the sheet had to be folded and put into an envelope, one had to write the name and address of sender and addressee on it, glue a stamp in the upper right-hand corner and find a mailbox. Add to this the inherently erratic nature of postal distribution; today's local newspaper runs a front-page headline which reads: 'Express letter took six days!' These limitations do not affect e-mail. For that reason, most of us send more e-letters than we used to send cellulose letters. E-mail is a blessing for the sender, but can be hell for the recipient.

Speed influences style and syntax. Many do not proofread their electronic correspondence. They start their letters, even to strangers, with an noncommittal, informal 'Hi!' or without any initial greeting whatsoever. (There are cultural differences here. The other day, I got an e-letter from a Japanese student, who solemnly apologised for writing to me 'without permission'.) The letters are often littered with half-baked sentences and bad grammar. Viewed in this way, e-mail can be located somewhere between the written and the oral, but if it more or less entirely replaces the old-fashioned letter, the culture as a whole will end with a deficit; it will have lost in quality whatever it has gained in quantity.

Speed also affects slow time adversely. It threatens to fill all the gaps. In the old days, a reply to a letter could take anything from a week to a month to reach the original sender. Nothing abnormal about that. So when one had put the envelope in the mailbox, one could return to work, sit down quietly and continue doing whatever one was doing for quite a while. This era is gone. Nowadays, we are expected to respond within hours, and, not infrequently, the same message is sent twice, perhaps with an interval of a day or less. The writer obviously believes one did not receive it the first time, since one has not yet replied.

This is not meant as a one-sided attack on fast time. Speed is excellent where it belongs. But it is contagious, and it has possibly serious side-effects. Unless we understand how speed functions, what it adds and what it removes, we are deprived of the opportunity to retain slowness where it is necessary.

We live in an era when the cigarette has replaced the pipe, cornflakes have replaced porridge, e-mail is replacing paper-based correspondence, and the 2-minute newsreel is one of the hottest products in the media field. The newspaper articles become shorter, the transitions in films more frequent, and the time each of us spends responding to an electronic letter is reduced in proportion to the number of e-letters we receive. The restless and shifting style of communication that was introduced with MTV has become an accurate image of the spirit of the age. Speed is an addictive drug: horrified, we watch ourselves groping for the fast-forward button in the cinema, the public loses interest in slow-moving sports; in my part of the world, ice skating and cross-country skiing have serious problems of recruitment and audience appeal, as people switch to more explosive sports such as ice hockey and downhill; we fill the slow gaps by talking in mobile phones when walking down a street or waiting for a traffic light to change; we damn the municipal transport authority when the tram is 5 minutes late, and we are still, after all these years, waiting for computers and Internet connections that are sufficiently fast. Everything moves faster now.

SPEED LEADS TO SIMPLIFICATION

One might also put it like this. Before the 1840s, one had to contact a portrait painter to have one's face saved for posterity. Royalty and commoners alike had to sit for ages in front of the painter. Then came the first, cumbersome photographic technology, the daguerreotype, which certainly was unsuitable for depictions of children, animals and other moving targets, since the time of exposure could last as long as an hour. Then came photography as we know it – incredibly, it has survived almost unchanged in form until it is only now about to be replaced by digital technology. ('Incredibly' because there has always been – at least for me – more than a hint of Jules Verne about the darkrooms with their red lights, chemical baths and drying lines.) But for many years, people dressed up in order to go to the photographers; in some towns, the outfitters were strategically located next door to the photographer; and afterwards, one waited a good while to see the result. Then the art of photography was democratised, and family fathers (and mothers) could take their 'snapshots' whenever it suited them, and exposed films became pictures in a matter of days. After the Second World War, the Polaroid camera was introduced, which automatically developed pictures in a minute; and, somewhat later, the first chains that promised to develop your film in an hour were established. At the time of writing, digital photography, launched in the second half of the 1990s, is finally making major inroads. The time taken to get from idea to image has gradually been reduced from several weeks to zero.

Seen in isolation, there is little cause to worry about these changes. But acceleration and compression are omnipresent, frequently with unintended consequences. One of the better parodies is Monty Python's 'competition' where the winner is the person who best succeeds in summarising Proust's *A la recherche du temps perdu* in 1 minute. ('And the winner is ... the girl with the biggest tits!') *Reader's Digest*, that pocket-sized magazine which specialises in publishing abridged and simplified versions of texts, was in this sense ahead of its time when it was launched in 1922. Since 1938, the magazine, which has a total global circulation of 28 million (!), has published its own book series. It consists, true to the ideology of the magazine, of radically shortened versions of existing books, ranging from John Grisham's latest blockbuster to Tolstoy's *War and Peace*. This is literature with an integrated fast forward button, tailored for an era with too much information and too little slow time. Some authors even claim that they enjoy these abridged versions of their own books, and allow the *Reader's Digest* to use their faces in its marketing programme.

SPEED CREATES ASSEMBLY LINE EFFECTS

Already at the first World Exhibition at Crystal Palace in London in 1851, where industrially produced goods were displayed in dazzling quantity and variation, the defenders of the traditional crafts objected that industrial goods were inferior. Quality requires time and highly developed personal skills, they argued, implying that the industrial form of mass production (which was still in its infancy) meant a vulgarisation of quality.

This attitude is far from uncommon; it can be encountered in many areas and can also be promoted with a variety of motivations. Elites have always tried to prevent the symbols of their elite status from being democratised. Industrially produced goods are cheaper and more accessible for common people than crafts were; for this very reason, there are groups in society that are virtually pre-programmed to claim that they are inferior merely because they are common. From a different perspective, one may reach the same conclusion (that is, a critical attitude to fast industrial production of goods) with environmental concerns as a starting-point, or by referring to the lifespan of products or that rather vaguer category called 'quality'. A common anecdote about the relationship between the USA and Great Britain is the one about lawns. 'How should we go about getting lawns as nice as the ones you have?' asks the impatient American. The Englishman answers, 'Start 400 years ago.'

Many products can be made faster and more efficiently without a necessary deterioration in quality. Plastic buckets and cars may be two examples. Other products are rather better off with labour-intensive, slow and thoughtful production – they last longer, taste better, sound better or whatever. There is something special about tailor-made clothing, especially adapted to *me* by another human being. With wine and cognac, slow maturation leads to improved quality, as is the case with many other foodstuffs, including beer, cheese and some kinds of meat.

There is no necessary connection between the duration of the act of cooking and quality (meaning good taste or nutritional value) in food. There are dishes that must simmer for hours before completion without thereby becoming particularly tasty or wholesome; one might think of, for example, certain English stews and a particularly nasty concoction of boiled mutton and cabbage that used to be a common Sunday dinner in Norway. Similarly, some hold the view that raw oysters with a drop of lemon (cooking time = zero) are a world-class culinary treat. Still, as a general rule, quality requires slow time in generous quantities with respect to food. Take poultry as a example. An average broiler in a country which has turned the production of meat into an industrial discipline on a par with car manufacturing, lives on an average a month. In my native country, the broiler will have been fed with growth-promoting nutrients for exactly a month when it reaches a gross weight of 1,100 grams, at which point it is decapitated, plucked and eventually grilled (always seasoned with the same mixture of salt and paprika powder) before being presented to the consumer. A few years ago, some people near a small town in the Oslo area discovered that if they allowed the chickens to lead more normal lives, their fat reserves were more amply developed and the meat, as a result, was juicier and tastier. They set up shop and began to produce chickens that were given regular food and, crucially, were allowed to live twice as long as the standard broiler. The result was a chicken that cost more than twice as much as usual, but which was also endowed with a radically different taste from the grilled industrial broilers most of us had grown up with.

A similar example on a larger scale concerns the North American Budweiser company's attempt to buy the Czech Budweiser brewery in the mid-1990s. The motivation for the takeover bid was easy enough to understand: the Czech brewery, which was large in a Central European context but a dwarf compared to the American beer factories, possessed the rights to the name Budweiser all over Europe. For this reason, the American product had to be sold under the label 'Bud' in Europe. Now, the two beers can be placed near either end on a scale measuring complexity in beer. US Budweiser looks like urine and tastes of carbonic acid with a tinge of bitterness added. The Czech namesake (also known as Budvar) is as golden, rich and aromatic as other Czech lagers, meaning that it belongs to the global premier division of beers. (Only about four countries count in the world league of beer; the Czech Republic is one of them.) Despite a generous offer, the American would-be buyers were turned down. The Czechs immediately saw that the production methods that would be introduced if they were to become part of the global Budweiser empire would entail a disastrous decline in quality. The demands for volume and speed were impossible to reconcile with a desire to make good beer. For that reason, there exists to this day two radically different Budweiser beers in the global market – a fast one, which is fine for quenching one's thirst in a hurry, and a slow one, which should be imbibed in quiet contemplation, and which can safely be served at room temperature.

Sometimes, the gains of speed and accessibility are greater than the losses, and sometimes the loss is imperceptible. It cannot, for example, be said for certain that there are droves of over-stressed people around who dream of an extra 10 minutes in the morning in order to replace their breakfast cereal with a bowl of porridge. Instant packets of various foodstuffs, from couscous and taco shells to Mediterranean pasta sauces or, for that matter, *sauce béarnaise*, give busy people the opportunity to prepare tasty meals that are nearly the real thing. If the alternative is nothing, because one rarely has the opportunity to spend hours cooking, this concept is far from being a bad idea. If speed and cost were to become the main criteria for choice of products, however, the result would be a net loss of richness and complexity in the culture as a whole. If enough of us stop tasting/smelling the difference between a cheap box wine and a vintage Bordeaux, cease to know that newly ground coffee beans give an entirely different result from the powder surrogate offered by Nestlé, fail to hear that Mahler's symphonies have a greater depth and richness than the latest pop songs, then the culture as a whole will have been impoverished. But puritanism is only for Puritans. Whenever I travel by air, I take great pleasure in drinking instant coffee although this is a product I normally regard with deep scepticism. The alternative is no coffee.

But speed has its costs, and sometimes (to think of it, quite often in the information age), nothing can be the best alternative to an instant version. If, say, you have an hour at your disposal for listening to classical music, and the alternatives are one full-length symphony and twelve five-minute summaries of various symphonies, the choice ought not to be difficult. The example is not absurd. Many of the bestselling classical records are 'summaries' or 'highlights'. Decontextualised snippets. And this is not as new as some might believe. In the inter-war years, Arthur Honegger composed his *Christmas Cantata*, where he cooked up a potpourri of familiar Christmas songs. Much has been heard before, and time is scarce. Composer and listener alike are anxious to hurry on.

SPEED LEADS TO A LOSS OF PRECISION

In the real old days, when contact with the outside world tended to be in the form of letters, correspondence took days or weeks. The rhythm of corresponding was slow and thoughtful. Illustrious individuals had their best letters collected in published works – one of our best sources to Marx's thought is his correspondence with Engels. Oscar Wilde's best essay, 'De Profundis', was actually a letter. It took Wilde two months to complete, and begins: 'Dear Bosie, After a long and fruitless waiting I have determined to write to you myself...'. It is hard to believe that anyone would be crazy enough to publish the 'selected e-mail' of a famous man or woman living today, but, naturally, I may be proven wrong.

Sloppiness and superficiality in correspondence notwithstanding, there are more serious consequences of acceleration. As a general rule, when one is required to act immediately, one does the first thing that comes to mind. (Anyone who has ever, say, pressed the red button or terminated a relationship in anger knows that the second or third thing often has a lot to recommend it.) Paul Virilio identifies a direct connection between acceleration and uncertainty.

The less slow time that remains to think decisions through, discuss and acquire a distanced overview, the greater is the risk for disastrous errors. The faster the territory changes, the less viable are the slow options. I shall leave apocalyptic fears to others. It is serious enough that acceleration in the media, in news coverage, social transformations and cultural changes, have resulted in a political practice virtually devoid of ideology, more dominated by media initiatives than by long-term thinking and clear models for society. Both populist types like Jörg Haider and designer politicians like Tony Blair are symptomatic of this trend. The slow ones are going out of business.

It is said about the legendary Swedish prime minister Tage Erlander that, one summer day in 1950, he was playing with a tape recorder when he heard on the radio that war had broken out in Korea. The war was not unanticipated, and many feared that it might eventually lead to a Third World War. What did Erlander do? He continued to play with his gadget, testing its microphone by thinking aloud about the war on tape. He was alone in the room. In spite of this slow reaction to a dramatic world event, nobody thought of criticising Erlander for indecision or failing to act immediately.

Even the 1950s was a fairly accelerated decade, and Erlander was, as a matter of fact, interrupted in his reflections by a journalist who wondered what he was going to do. But today everything moves much faster. Decisions have to be taken at the speed of light, otherwise, one is squeezed out by those who act faster. This principle is as valid in the global financial market as in politics or marketing. Since Haider has already been mentioned: it took the governments of all EU states less than 24 hours to implement sanctions against Austria when, in the winter of 2000, a party with an unpleasant smell became a partner in a government coalition there. Suppose time had moved only a bit more slowly: in that case, half the EU governments would presumably have had second thoughts about the sanctions, realising that other means would be more appropriate. (And suppose time had moved even more slowly: in that case, Haider would probably never have been in power in the first place.) The domino effects in the global financial markets, further, now take place at incredible speeds – a ripple in Hong Kong reverberates immediately in Singapore, spreading repercussions to LA and London literally before anyone has the time to raise an eyebrow.

These are just some examples of the tyranny of the moment.

We are dealing with a phenomenon which is much more encompassing than 'media society', a cliché that has been around for decades already. But it must also be said that the mass media – especially radio and television – are important trendsetters and virus carriers concerning speed. Now, journalism has always been a profession characterised by speed. The notion of today's paper is both a symbol and a sign of modernity. It is worth nothing if it is not *current*. Typically, the newspapers had their major breakthrough in the late eighteenth century, at the same time that clocks began to be used to monitor work; which was also the same period that the French and American Revolutions introduced their individualistic ideals of freedom and the Industrial Revolution began to transform labour. There was now a critical mass of people, especially in the major cities, who felt an acute need to keep up to date with contemporary events. Then, as now, a newspaper was ephemeral. Its lifespan was exactly one day.

Other media are faster. Radio and television can update their content any time, and this is also the case with the media which will probably, within a few years, replace the newspapers, namely electronic publications based on text. (In this field, technological change happens so fast that there is little point in attempting to make accurate predictions, but it is worth noticing that a 'promising prototype' in late 2000 had a passing similarity to a tabloid newspaper, but it was being updated as frequently as the user wished with 'electronic ink'.)

It makes little sense to talk about the lifespan of an Internet newspaper: any item survives only until the staff have managed to update or replace it. The faster they are updated, the better their reputation, the more hits they get, and the more sponsorship. An average reader of the leading electronic newspaper in Norway – the only newspaper, incidentally, that does not have a paper version – spends 45 seconds browsing the paper. News addicts go there several times a day, especially during dramatic events (civil wars, hostage dramas, football championships...). This kind of media instils a new rhythm and a new restlessness, and – importantly – new routines in the consumption of news. During the annual negotiations between the trade unions and the employers' organisation, strikes are a threat which often become a reality on a small or large scale in Norway. Once I sat at my computer late at night during these lengthy negotiations, and the next morning I was due to fly to another city for a conference. If the negotiations broke down, SAS personnel would go on strike, with obvious consequences for my immediate plans. I therefore checked the Internet newspapers regularly in order to follow the latest developments. As bedtime approached, all the main electronic newspapers informed me that agreement was still not reached, that the negotiations continued, and that the tired and hungry negotiators had ordered pizza. Fine, but my evening of work had been seriously disrupted. If the electronic newspapers had not existed, the paper I delivered the next day (for there was no strike after all) might have been better.

The leader of an Internet company created a minor stir among Scandinavian journalists in 2000 when she took the liberty of thinking aloud about quality control and source use in Internet journalism. Her view was that Internet journalists had to work so fast that they rarely had time to check their sources. Therefore, this burden was transferred to the *reader*, as befits the brave new world of informational democracy.

When one comes across rubbish of this calibre, it is difficult to know whether to burst into tears or cynical laughter. Does she really mean that I should travel to Kosovo and start digging up graves in order to expose NATO lies about the extent of genocide? Should I personally phone Victoria Beckham to ask her about her recent whereabouts, since I harbour a vague suspicion that my local web site might not have got all the details right? And do I really have to watch all the unspeakably depressing football games of my national team, just to get a confirmation of a fact everyone is aware of, namely that the national media are unable to offer a detached description of them?

In a sense, the answer is yes, and this is where reality calls a halt to any initial merriness. A friend who used to work for the leading national Internet newspaper says that his main reason for leaving the job (for another, less glamorous and less well-paid position) was exactly this: the only point was to beat the others, to have your news published as fast as possible. Any corrections could be added any time, so don't worry.

Ignacio Ramonet is chief editor of the excellent, and not least slow, monthly *Le Monde Diplomatique*. In his book *La Tyrannie de la communication*, he is inclined towards a more worried than humorous attitude to the consequences of increased speed in journalism. At the outset, he states that never before have people had access to more information, but this does not mean that they have also become better informed. One important cause is speed, although Ramonet also looks at ownership and self-censorship. Speed, combined with increased quantities of information on offer at any given moment, leads both to heightened competition and weakened editorial treatment. He quotes the justly famous journalist Ryszard Kapúscinski, who claims that editors no longer fuss over the 'credibility' of a story, but rather judge its merits on whether or not it is sufficiently 'interesting'. That a story should have a wider societal relevance is not a criterion in this regard, and characteristically, the greatest global news stories in the couple of years preceding Ramonet's book (published in 1999) were the death of Princess Diana and the affair between Bill Clinton and Monica Lewinsky. Ramonet shows that there is no space for complexity in this overheated brand of journalism. (Kipling, it must in all fairness be added, said this a hundred years earlier, referring to the American penchant for speed.) A simple good/bad contrast is all that can be crammed into the decreasing number of consumer seconds journalists have at their disposal. This is a main reason why it was so difficult to give the civil war in Rwanda proper coverage, but it also sheds interesting light on the rise of populist politics in several European countries, with their simple slogans and easy fixes.

Although the scarcity of time at the receiving end may be an argument for the increased speed of news turnover, there is an interesting dialectic here in that hardly any other profession (apart from politicians) has suffered a similar decline in public esteem in the last couple of decades. In the USA, in Britain, France and Scandinavia, journalists are distrusted by a majority of the people questioned by pollsters. A few decades ago, Ramonet muses, journalism was a profession associated with personal integrity, courage and selfless search for truth; cartoon heroes like Superman (Clark Kent), Spiderman (Peter Parker) and Tintin are all journalists by profession. This would not have been viable today. The Enlightenment equation information = freedom = democracy is difficult to uphold when the criteria for journalistic coverage are immediate appeal and fast publishing.

SPEED DEMANDS SPACE

This is one of the most general principles of speed. The faster cars drive, the more lanes one needs for the same number of cars. When it is impossible to expand the available space and the number of vehicles grows, speed decreases. Information does not require space in the same sense as cars, but it does require time. The great scarce resource for all purveyors of information – from advertisers to authors – is *the attention of others*. When an ever increasing amount of information has to be squeezed into the relatively constant amount of time each of us has at our disposal, the span of attention necessarily decreases. Television has paved the way here. As viewers get accustomed to taking in more and more compressed information, it can be compressed even further. Early in the 1990s, a study of California schoolchildren revealed that their attention span in class lasted, on an average, 7 minutes. They were accustomed to the rhythm created by commercial breaks on television. Here, it seems, educators are faced with a real challenge: how to design teaching methods that do not require more than 7 minutes of continuous time between the breaks! In some areas, this could be done. Rote learning of strong verbs, for example. In other areas, the solution must evidently be less straightforward.

One way of obtaining a snippet of people's attention thus consists in making certain that time is fast and cut into conveniently short lengths. Everyone has 8 seconds to spare; but who has two years? (This may be the time required to understand the history of Western philosophy.) Another, related technique consists in *filling all the gaps*. The WAP telephone technology makes it possible to read e-mail, news and bus schedules in the lift, on the beach or while playing soccer with one's children. In the spring of 2000, a new WAP telephone was launched with an integrated MP3 player. This means that in the breaks between scanning written information or talking on the phone, one can use the telephone to listen to music. This ensures that the empty and boring pauses; the gaps, the time that might have been used for free-floating slow thoughts, are eradicated. WAP as such is probably a passing fad, but the Japanese equivalent, i-mode, had an incredible 14 million users in late 2000 – a year after its initial launching. *New Scientist* notes, near the beginning of a feature section from autumn 2000, that at least 20 Japanese acquired an i-mode phone 'in the minute it's taken you to read this far'.

The cellphone technology of the near future will make it possible to identify the user's exact location. This could turn the phone into a device which efficiently fills the few gaps that are left in a busy urban person's life. There is still a gap of maybe a couple of minutes between leaving the car and entering the first shop in the mall. Soon, one will hear a beep from the cellphone upon approaching the mall entrance, and onscreen information will flash forth: 'Special offer today at Sainsbury's: New Zealand lamb £2.99, 30 feet ahead and to the left.' This is an extension of the logic that has brought us the petrol nozzle ad and the shopping trolley ad (it was only a year ago that I noticed that the trolley handle at my local supermarket had suddenly tripled in width, to make room for advertising).

Those who offer information, and our numbers are on the rise, fight over the vacant seconds in the lives of others. The greater the number of information pedlars, the fewer seconds users have for each of them. The senders certainly cannot use coercion, in this age of libertarian fundamentalism, and so they must be smart. Does anyone still wonder why the number of information consultants grew exponentially during the 1990s?

SPEED IS CONTAGIOUS

This holds true in the media, as elsewhere. The fastest media, at the moment television and Internet newspapers, are being imitated by the printed media. The articles become shorter and shorter, with clearer 'messages' and less analysis. Dedicated news channels on radio, for their part, boast that they update their news every hour, while the WAP format epitomises everything that is fast in contemporary mass communication. WAP phones and similar devices have a 'screen' which is about twice as large as the display of an ordinary mobile phone, as well as direct access to limited sectors of the Internet. One can, for example, check the stock exchange rates, the evening's cinema programme, the news headlines and the e-mail on a WAP telephone, and the superbrief news items are updated virtually continuously. In the bad old days, one had to wait until the TV news in the early evening for an update.

It is not unlikely that this kind of technology will become widespread. In a situation with an information surplus, everyone has 10 seconds to spare, but very few have a whole minute. This gives a competitive edge to the fastest and most compact media. A general rule of the information revolution is that in a 'free and fair' competition between a slow and a fast version of 'the same thing', the fast version wins. The question is what gets lost on the way. The short answer to this question is *context* and *understanding*; the longer one involves *credibility*. It is hard enough to edit a credible daily newspaper, which, among other things, attracts readers through being first with the latest. But, as a senior editor of a major broadsheet mentioned to me during a fast and fragmentary conversation on a streetcorner: just imagine being managing editor for the WAP edition of a newspaper, which demands continuous updating! One would scarcely have the time to type the news before it was published and therefore in need of revision. This situation is just around the corner as I write this.

Ramonet claims that during the last 30 years, more information has been produced than during the previous 5,000 years! He illustrates the point with an example: 'A single copy of the Sunday edition of the *New York Times* contains more information than a cultivated person in the eighteenth century would consume during a lifetime.'

I have no way of knowing whether performances of Beethoven's sixth symphony, the idyllic *Pastoral* symphony, are much faster today than the performances of 200 years ago. But as already mentioned, plays have accelerated very noticeably during the twentieth century. A political scientist recently studied the development of the annual financial debate in the Norwegian parliament, comparing the speed of speech in selected years from 1945 to 1995. He shows that the members of parliament spoke at an average velocity of 584 phonemes per minute in 1945. In 1980, the number of sounds had risen to 772, and in 1995 it had reached 863. In other words, the average politician spoke 50 per cent faster in 1995 than his or her predecessors did in the mid-1940s.

Or one could put it like this: it is as if one lives in an old, venerable but slightly dilapidated house and decides to refurbish the bathroom. Having finally done this, a poorer but hopefully happier person following a budgetary deficit worthy of the United Nations, one discovers for the first time that the kitchen is really quite rundown. So one begins to tear out the old kitchen fittings, and soon enters a new frustrating round of phone calls to plumbers and masons. Then one is bound to discover, almost immediately, how old and worn the hall is, and really, wouldn't it be a terrific idea to give the living room a coat of paint and a new floor? Speed is contagious in an analogous way.

If one gets used to speed in some areas, the desire for speed will tend to spread to new domains. Five minutes spent waiting for the bus lasts longer the faster the airport express train takes you from the terminal to the bus stop. As computer networks have become faster, many of us have grown accustomed to an Internet connection where waiting time is in principle, and often in practice, minimal. Still, we will not rest content until the web pages are accessed the very same moment we press the button. Two seconds of waiting time today is as unacceptable as 10 seconds would have been a couple of years ago.

This principle has a general validity. If the plane from Oslo to Copenhagen takes 40 minutes, 15 minutes' delay makes a lot of difference. If, on the other hand, one chooses to take the boat, which takes an evening and a night to cross the Skagerrak, 15 minutes lost or saved makes little difference, since the rhythm of the boat militates against petty time-saving schemes. Other activities can wait. Fast time, in other words, is contagious both between persons and between life domains.

GAINS AND LOSSES TEND TO EQUAL EACH OTHER OUT

In 1965, the engineer Gordon Moore spelled out the principle that has come to be known as 'Moore's Law'. It states that the capacity (read: speed) of microprocessors is doubled every 18 months. (Recently, it has been supplemented by 'Gilder's Law', which states that the transmission speed – bandwidth – on the Net is doubled every year.) So far, Moore has been right. However, a computer scientist at my university supplemented Moore with 'Knut's Law'. It states that Moore's law is correct, but that computer software doubles in complexity and size every 16 months. According to Knut, then, the daily chores performed by any computer nowadays take *longer* than before.

Knut is obviously a witty man, and he exaggerates. (Actually his law reminds me of a newspaper story from a few years back, on the assumed health benefits of jogging. It noted that people who jog do live longer than others – on average, exactly as much longer as the time they spend jogging.) But in a general sense, Knut is right. Allow me to illustrate with a few examples from my own computer world, which is called Macintosh. The first version of the word processor MacWrite, launched in 1984, took a little more than 50 Kb of disk space (disks back then, remember, took all of 400 Kb). The program I am using to write this book, WriteNow 4 (that is, the 1994 version), takes 348 Kb of disk space. The latest version of the world's most popular word processor, which is Microsoft Word, requires 5.1 Mb, in other words well over 5,000 Kb. And for the program to function properly, a heap of additions are needed. Some of them are shared with the sister programs Excel and PowerPoint. Altogether, Microsoft's office package requires more than 100 Mb, and most people install all programs.

In the old days, that is a little over a dozen years ago, the total capacity of an ordinary hard disk was 20 Mb. We felt we had a lot of space back then, we who had grown up with computers without hard disks! We might have a word processor such as MacWrite (50 Kb), a presentation program like More (384 Kb in the last and best version) and a spreadsheet such as CricketGraph (200 Kb) at our disposal, and were able to perform the same tasks that an average user of Microsoft Word now needs more than 100 Mb of disk space to perform. Naturally, he or she also needs a much faster computer than we could even dream of at the time.

So the software has been improved? That depends on what one is after. Personally I prefer the simple and stable programs. They are easy to learn and straightforward to relate to, and although I write hundreds of pages every year, I never seem to need more than what humble WriteNow is able to offer. Yes, Word does make it possible to make tables of contents and fancy templates, and to run a number of functions automatically through macros; but in my experience, it is easier to tailor documents to one's special needs as one goes along. The simpler a computer program is, the less time and energy is spent on relating to the actual technology and trying to read the thoughts of the programmers, and more concentration can be expended on the task at hand. The larger and more complex a program is, the greater the risk of crashes and breakdowns. Irritating macro viruses have in recent years become widespread among computer users, but only among Word users.

This is to do with too much complexity of the wrong kind. Increased speed does not even necessarily make us more efficient – a point to which I shall return later. The magazine *WIRED* ran a story a few years ago about the new CEO of mighty Sun Microsystems, and how he wanted to improve the efficiency of his staff. He came up with several ideas, but one in particular took the computer addicts on the staff by surprise. Now, many of the employees routinely made transparencies for use in external and internal presentations of what they were up to. As an aid, they had loads of templates, illustrations, suggestions and previously used presentations lying around on the shared hard disks of the company. While working on a particular pre-sentation, people would browse these files to look for ideas, suitable templates, etc. The CEO found out that there were altogether 12.9 gigabytes of PowerPoint stuff on the servers. He deleted everything. From now on, the staff had to make their own presentations from scratch. And indeed, they now worked more efficiently, and spent less time on each transparency than before.

TECHNOLOGICAL CHANGE LEADS TO UNPREDICTED SIDE-EFFECTS

All technology has unintended consequences, and whenever one gets more of a particular kind of technology, the result is not necessarily 'more of the same'. It could just as well be 'something entirely different'. One telling example is the transition from single-channel (or, at any rate, two- or three-channel) television to multi-channel television operated by a remote control. In most European countries, this change has taken place since around 1980. National television is a fantastic tool for propaganda – or, put differently, it can create a very powerful, shared national identity. It communicates directly, simultaneously and emotionally to literates as well as illiterates. It synchronises large segments of the population, and presents a particular version of reality to all – from Leningrad to Vladivostok, or from Munich to Kiel. Research has indicated that the dialect variation in several European countries was reduced during the twentieth century thanks to national radio and television, where a few nationally acknowledged variants were dominant.

After a generation of single-channel television, satellite TV was introduced in remote Norway in 1983. To begin with, dedicated satellite channels such as Sky and Super were dominant, and the field was still so scantily populated that certain of Sky's video jockeys were able to achieve megastar status in some European countries, since a large percentage of the target group followed them. (Anyone remember Pat Sharp?) There were only a few alternatives. Eventually, TV viewers got access to new Norwegian channels (around five or six at the latest count), in addition to a growing selection of satellite channels. Not everyone has access to everything, and many of the channels operate on the basis of subscriptions. Nonetheless, media research shows that the old national monopoly, the Norwegian poor cousin of the BBC, has lost its grip on the population. The good old days when the majority of the population gathered around the screen when the evening news was on, are gone never to return. In other words: television (and radio) functioned in an immensely integrating manner, creating a shared field of discourse on a national level, so long as it was dominated by one or a few, often state-controlled channels. Then we got a little more of the same technology (more channels, and some more, and some more still), and suddenly television no longer creates integration, but fragmentation.

We have still only seen the beginning. Digital TV, which at the time of writing has graduated from the grapevine to the pipeline, entails that each household can in principle develop its own, unique pattern of viewing. I can watch jazz concerts and poetry recitals until I fall over, while my neighbour can concentrate his attention on classical Westerns, only interrupted by weather reports presented by young and beautiful women.

It is easy to find examples from cultural history to indicate that the introduction of new technology has led to consequences other than those anticipated. I have already suggested that some of the technologies of speed, intended to boost efficiency, may have grave side-effects – and that it cannot even be taken for granted that they do boost efficiency. This is going to be a major theme later, and I shall leave it for now. But take eyeglasses, for example. Although their exact origin is unknown, the first known reference to optical lenses is from Roger Bacon, writing in 1268. Spectacles made it possible for learned persons, monks and others, to continue reading for many years after their eyesight had begun to deteriorate. For several centuries, only convex glasses, to aid farsightedness (hyperopia), existed. This is the common form of eyesight deterioration among people above 40. The importance of this modest invention for the Renaissance and the beginning of the modern era should not be underestimated. The cumulative growth in knowledge was boosted enormously when members of the learned community of Europe could continue to expand their fields of learning throughout their lives.

Far-fetched example? Perhaps, but there are also excellent examples of wide-ranging unintended consequences of technological change to be found in mainstream cultural history. The clock, as noted earlier, was originally constructed to synchronise prayer times for monks working the fields during the day; today, it is a pillar of the modern way of life, and has become indispensable for industrial production, mass communication and large chunks of people's everyday life everywhere. When movable type was invented by Gutenberg, scarcely anyone thought that it would be decisive in the development of democracy and nationalism. And neither Gottlieb Daimler nor Henry Ford would have expected the car to lead to inner-city decay since it moved residential areas to the suburbs and shops to consumption reservations near major highways. On a minor note, it might be added that nobody would have thought, when commercial air traffic was introduced in a small way in the 1930s – as a luxurious treat for the wealthy and powerful – that inter-continental flights would be a backbone in the migration process from poor to rich countries.

New technology cannot be used for anything at all, but it is also never known how it will be used. Technological changes, no matter how dazzling, are always put to use by particular societies with particular needs. They also bring subtle, but often highly conse-quential side-effects with them. Writing, as mentioned in the previous chapter, impairs the faculty of memory.

Who would have believed, in the mid-1990s, that the most active users of mobile phones would be adolescents, and that they largely use them to send SMS messages in order to stay in touch with their friends hour by hour? (At the latest count, 9 billion SMS messages are sent annually in the world, a billion of them in Germany alone.) When personal computers were first marketed around 1980, reasonably well-informed journalists wrote in a deeply serious mode how they would be used to make shopping lists and inventories of the contents of the freezer. The new information technology that lurks in the background of this entire book, is still at a trial stage, and there is no way of knowing how it will be put to use in three, five or 20 years. It is nonetheless easy to see *some* consequences of information technology: it removes distance, shortens time and fills the gaps with cascades of information. Like the car and the jet plane, new information technology leads to acceleration and demands for further information, until time – seen as duration – approaches zero. But as complexity increases, so do the side-effects. Roads, for instance, have a curious tendency to be filled by cars, no matter how many lanes they have at their disposal. And a given computer network may function well for 1,000 users who run e-mail software and Netscape/Explorer, but badly for 10,000 users who are up to the same thing; just as it would function badly if the 1,000 users demanded transmissions of high-resolution video film in real time. Just as traffic jams occur worldwide in the rush hour, annoying delays and jams occur on the Net.

The proposed solutions are the same in both cases: we require more capacity and higher speed, as if that would solve anything in the long run. But let us not forget how happy we were when we finally got hard disks with a storage capacity of all of 20 Mb; at that time, we then had no idea that those devices would be ripe for the museum in less than four years.

The contagious nature of speed, and its intimate relationship to efficiency as a value in itself, is brought out clearly in a well-known story which exists in many versions. In the variant told by Heinrich Böll, a German tourist visits Spain and discovers, to his horror, a Spaniard dozing in the shade of a tree on the beach. The German approaches the man, a fisherman, and lectures him on the virtues of efficiency: 'If you had gone out fishing now instead of wasting your time, he explains, you might have caught three times as much fish and bought yourself a better boat.' Eventually, he fantasises, the Spaniard might employ others and build a factory. He could become a rich man! 'What for?', asks the Spaniard. 'Well', says the German, 'you could have gone into early retirement, living off the profits and spent your days dozing on the beach.' 'That', says the Spaniard before turning over, 'is exactly what I am doing.'

Something has run out of control. Time-saving technology has made time more scarce than ever. The wealth of available information has not made most of us more enlightened, but less enlightened. In the next chapter, I shall explain how this can be, and approach the question of what this 'something' is that seems to be out of control.

5 Exponential Growth

When I described Madame de T.'s night, I recalled the well-known equation from one of the first chapters of the textbook of existential mathematics: the degree of speed is directly proportional to the intensity of forgetting.

(Milan Kundera, *Slowness*)

The most famous myth about the invention of chess is located to Persia in a remote and misty era. (It is almost certainly wrong: chess was probably invented in India in the sixth century AD.) The king of the wealthy Persian empire loved games and intellectual challenges. One day he had exhausted the possibilities inherent in the games at hand, and ordered the sharpest mind of the court to conjure up a new game that would surpass everything he had seen thus far. After a while he was presented with a stylised war game, with a board measuring eight times eight squares in alternating black and white colours, and with two sets of pieces, one in each colour, carved in wood. The pieces depicted soldiers and officers; the infantry ('pawns') were numerous, but there were only a couple of officers of each rank. Naturally, each warring side had only one king and queen, and they were the most important pieces in the game. For some reason, the queen had a greater range than the king, but it was only when the king was besieged that the game was over.

The Persian king was very pleased, and offered the inventor the fee he required. 'I will not ask for much, my lord', the man replied modestly, 'just one grain of wheat for the first square of the board, two for the second, four for the third, eight for the fourth, sixteen for the fifth and so on, until we reach the sixty-fourth and final square.' 'That you shall have', said the king in relief, saving his treasury from depletion of gold and brilliant stones; and then his mathematicians began to calculate how much wheat they would have to fetch from the stores.

They were surprised. For a while, it seemed as if the expense would be very modest for the king. The ten first squares yielded barely enough wheat for a porridge meal for the inventor and his family (see Figure 5.1a). Then, the numbers seemed to grow more rapidly – albeit in reality, they continued to grow at the same rate as from the

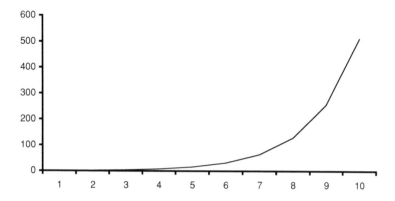

Figure 5.1a Number of wheat grains for the inventor of chess: the first 10 squares

beginning, but they quickly grew very much larger. Twice as large for each new square on the board. The tenth square was worth 512 grains, the eleventh 1024. The fifteenth square was worth 16,384 grains, the twentieth more than half a million (see Figure 5.1b). The twenty-sixth square was valued at more than 33 million grains of wheat, the thirty-first more than a billion (see Figure 5.1c).

It had to end in disaster. Long before the courtly mathematicians had calculated the grain values of all 64 squares of the chess board,

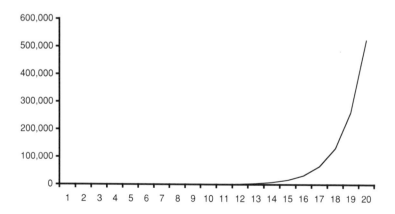

Figure 5.1b Number of wheat grains for the inventor of chess: the first 20 squares

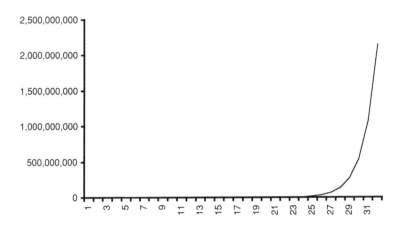

Figure 5.1c Number of wheat grains for the inventor of chess: the first 32 squares

they realised that the king owed the inventor of the game many times the world's total wheat harvest.

The mythical inventor of chess was clearly also the inventor of exponential mathematics. The principle of the most common exponential function is doubling for each step or time interval. The actual

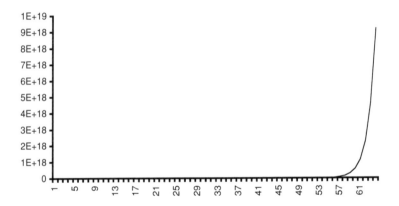

Note: 1E+18 is 1 followed by 18 zeros, etc.

Figure 5.1d Number of wheat grains for the inventor of chess: all 64 squares rate of growth, in other words, is even, but the numerical growth follows a low curve before it suddenly rises towards the ceiling. As Figure 5.1 a–d indicates, the growth curve is pretty steep even if we look at the first ten steps, but it still seems harmless since the numbers are so small. Compared with the value for the sixty-fourth and final square, the value for the thirty-second square – a mere 2,147,483,648 grains – is insignificant. The king's debt for the last square amounted to 9,223,372,036,854,780,000 grains.

Many current tendencies seem susceptible to descriptions by way of roughly exponential growth curves with varying rates of doubling. Let me hazard some guesses at the outset: air traffic since the Second World War, global population growth over the last 200 years, the turnover at the NASDAQ stock exchange since its foundation, the number of Internet servers in the world since 1995, the traffic on the Internet since 1991, the size of Microsoft Word since 1985, the average number of system extensions on a Macintosh since 1984, the number of murders an average American teenager has seen on television since 1950, the number of academic journals published since 1950, the number of detergent brands in the world since 1950, the number of television channels since 1980...

EXPONENTIAL GROWTH IS EVEN AND MAY SEEM UNDRAMATIC FOR A LONG TIME

An example similar to the origin myth of chess, but which is closer to contemporary concerns, is this:

Two bacteria colonised a bottle. They bred at average speed, and a sticky, brown layer of beer covered the bottom of the bottle, which stood in the shade in a tropical country and had a constant temperature of slightly below 30°C. Under these circumstances, it took the bacteria 1 minute to double in number. When the first minute was gone, there were thus 4 bacteria, then 8, 16, 32 and so on. (Eventually some begin to die, which makes the calculations more complicated.) It took them months just to cover the bottom of the bottle. When this was accomplished, the population growth took off. When an eighth of the bottle was full, the brightest mathematicians among the bacteria had calculated that the bottle was faced with a disastrous population explosion. Not many listened to them. When, a little more than 2 minutes later, the bottle was half full, many began to worry. They organised petitions and demonstrations, carrying banners and shouting angry slogans, demanding the authorities do something to avert a terrible catastrophe. The politicians replied: 'Don't worry, there is plenty of space.'

This allegory of the population explosion has a long prehistory, beginning in 1798, when Thomas Robert Malthus published his *An Essay on Population*. This was at the very beginning of what would later be seen as a period of explosive population growth, and, whatever one's views on Malthus, one must at least concede that he was ahead of his time. According to Malthus, food production grew arithmetically, that is by simple addition: 1, 2, 3, 4, 5... Population, on the contrary, had a tendency to grow geometrically (or exponentially), that is 1, 2, 4, 8, 16, etc. For this reason, famine would occur unless one took steps to reduce population growth. Malthus, a cleric, naturally recommended sexual abstinence.

Malthus's thoughts have been deeply influential in both politics and science for 200 years. Darwin's theory of natural selection hinges on a Malthusian mechanism of 'natural growth', while Marx, who admired Darwin, castigated Malthus in extremely strong terms even by his own standards (he once characterised him as 'the baboon Malthus'). In a general way, his model of population growth still underlies international discussions about population growth, and the arguments have not changed significantly since Marx's time: Malthus's detractors point out that social distribution and technological factors influence the population size a given territory can sustain.

We may assume, with Malthus, that each couple on earth has on average four children who survive. This is the number necessary for a simple exponential curve. Let us, further, assume that the span from birth to own children lasts on an average 30 years. A certain village, we may call it Filthy Brook, was founded by two couples in 1798, on the same day as Malthus published his theory. Total population: four persons. A little later, let us say in 1805, they each have four children. Total population: twelve. After 30 years, the eight children have married their neighbours, and each couple is bringing up four children each. Total population: $12 + (4 \times 4) = 28$. Then the elderly die. Total population is now reduced to 24. Thirty years later, that is in 1865, the second generation are dead, but their 16 children have married each other and have given birth to four children each.

Total population is now 24 – 8 + (8 × 4) = 48. Then another 30 years pass, with loss of grandparents, new marriages and new children, and the population of Filthy Brook in 1895 is 48 – 8 + (16 × 4) = 168. It now begins to look like a village proper. Filthy Brook gets its first grocery and a post office. Ninety years on, in 1985, another three generations have passed. There are now a total of 896 inhabitants. It is easy to support everybody, and the village remains something less than a small town. (The post office is nevertheless closed down in this period, for reasons which will not be discussed here.) But, the mathematicians of the village say, imagine the situation in 2195! We will then have a population of 229,376. Not much will then be left of our cosy English village.

On a global scale, this kind of population growth is naturally a recipe for crowding in the long run. There is nonetheless no agreement regarding what 'the long run' should be taken to mean here, that is what is the upper limit for the planet's sustainability, and people in general seem to rather enjoy living close together. Rat psychologists should take notice. The world may still be less crowded than many worried Malthusians believe. At the moment, if we assume that every person alive were brought to Wales, each individual would have 4 square metres at his or her exclusive disposal. Assuming the existence of a reasonable housing scheme with efficient use of space, there might even be space for a café or two.

For many thousands of years, humanity grew very slowly. It has been estimated that the Earth was able to support roughly 8 million people altogether before the agricultural revolution. This number is certainly subject to debate, but it is a fact that the global population at the dawn of the agricultural revolution is estimated at about 5 million. The first billion was reached only in 1800. Another 130 years went before the second billion mark was passed, 30 years between 2 billion and 3 billion, and 15 years from 3 billion to 4 billion, reached in 1975. In 1987, the global population was 5 billion, and we had only just become accustomed to this figure when, twelve years later, it was announced that citizen of the world number 6 billion had just been born, probably in India or China. If the present rate of growth continues, the world's population will continue to double every 40 years. (There are twice as many people alive today as when I was born.) In that case, global population will be 12 billion in 2040 and 48 billion in 2120. In some parts of the world, the rate of doubling is much faster (Africa: 24 years, Asia: 34 years). Almost no matter what time scale is employed, the growth curve of the global population will tend to point skywards on the right. But it is beginning to flatten out. The interval between 4 billion and 5 billion was twelve years; the same as the interval between 5 billion and six billion.

What these examples indicate is that an even development of exponential growth may seem undramatic for quite a while – it may even be perceived as modest and wholesome – before suddenly changing character and shooting upwards. When this leap takes place, a qualitative change occurs with the *content*. After a while, the small village Filthy Brook is a small town, and before one knows it, it is a city. The modest games-maker at the King's court is suddenly transformed into a cunning megalomaniac.

EXPONENTIAL GROWTH CREATES SCARCITY OF SPACE

This chapter does not really deal with chess games, bacteria or population growth. I took the liberty of appropriating a few minutes of the readers' time on these examples in order to introduce a particular line of reasoning. The topic is the surplus of information and the uncontrolled growth in the available quantity of information, and some of the results of this tendency. In an earlier chapter I wrote that whereas there was formerly a scarcity of information, there is now too much of it. If it is correct that, in the course of the past 30 years, humanity has produced as much information as in the previous 5,000 years, we are talking about a very steep curve.

A growing number of messages are fighting over forever shrinking vacant spaces. An obvious result is that each of us has to spend a decreasing amount of time on each piece of information. The most widely-read newspaper edition in Norway is the one published on the last Wednesday before Easter. This has nothing to do with quality, but with the simple fact that this country has five consecutive newspaper-free days during Easter. It can also be assumed that when there were fewer television channels, people watched TV in a more calm and continuous mode. When there were fewer professional journals, readers spent more time on each article. When there were fewer CDs on the shelf, one played each of them more often and became more familiar with each piece of music. When there were fewer books...

The compression of information into decreasing time spans also entails changes on the sender side. The people who make TV programmes nowadays, for example, are perfectly aware that they are making them for a group of spectators armed with a remote control in their right hand, ready to zap to a competing channel as soon the temperature of the programme falls. When Ted Turner launched CNN in 1982, he wanted briefer commercials to match his 2-minute 'headline news' programmes. The 30-second commercial, which had been regarded as ultra-fast when it was introduced in 1971, was suddenly sluggish. Turner hired the media consultant Tony Schwartz, who immediately shortened the 30 seconds to 8, then to 5 seconds. In an interview, Schwartz recently boasted that he could make 3-second commercials which would outcompete all of these, and offered examples of such commercials.

After a while, viewers grow accustomed to the new tempo. One of the most striking aspects of feature films from the 1950s, at least for us who live in the 2000s, is how unbelievably slow they are, with slowly unfolding dialogues, lingering scenes with crashing waves and sunsets, people who seem to be looking at each other for many seconds, seemingly without anything better to do. Even though the audience of a cinema is not equipped with a remote control or a fast forward button, the expectations created by watching the TV screen affect the rhythm of cinema spectatorship: as much as possible ought to happen as fast as possible; the more, the better.

Speed is not just contagious; it is addictive as well. (Unlike nearly everything else to do with consumption of information, cinema attendance is decreasing globally, correlated with the spread of video machines. Does this have anything to do with the presence/absence of the fast forward button?) Just as it is easier to make people increase their consumption than to make them reduce it, it is easier to increase than to reduce the tempo of information transmission. Speed is a narcotic.

SIDE-EFFECTS BECOME DOMINANT

This is about too much complexity of the wrong kind. Friedrich Engels, factory manager and Marxist (he was actually the first Marxist, as Karl Marx's long-standing patron and collaborator), once wrote about how quantitative changes are, at particular points, turned into qualitative changes. This principle was developed in one of his most vilified books, the study of 'the dialectics of nature' where he offered a theory of change in nature. The book, published posthumously in the inter-war years, is indeed a curious read. But the principle of the transformation of quantity into quality deserves a second look, as long as it is applied where it belongs (which is not the evolution of species). A given system produces more and more and more of the same, but suddenly, one gets something entirely different instead of more of the same. This frequently happens without anybody noticing.

One may do three things at the same time and do three things well. One may do six things at the same time and do six things well. Some may even do twelve things at the same time and do twelve things well. Then they get a thirteenth task, and suddenly they perform thirteen tasks badly. This is the essence of the transformation of quantity into quality. Even growth takes place for a long while without dramatic consequences, but suddenly a threshold value is reached, and as a result the entire system flips into something different, changing character completely.

A classic example from anthropology are the 'pig cycles' among the Tsembaga of Highland New Guinea. The Tsembaga grow tubers and vegetables, and raise pigs. The porcine population increases evenly. As it grows, women and children (who are responsible for the pigs) must go further and further from the village to herd them, risking assaults from enemy peoples, and at the same time, the pigs do increasing harm to the crops. After a particular number of pig generations, the Tsembaga have reached a point where keeping pigs is no longer an asset but a liability. They then slaughter nearly all of them and enter into a complex ritual process of warfare and re-settlement. (There are simpler solutions available, but that is not the point here.)

Another example is narrated by the system theorist Gregory Bateson (1904–80). His allegory describes a fantastic horse developed by the sharpest minds in genetics, *the polyploid horse*. This horse was twice as long, twice as wide and twice as tall as a normal horse.

Of course, its weight was eight times that of an ordinary horse. It was unable to support its own weight in an upright position, for its skeleton was only four times as thick as that of an ordinary horse. The inner organs were continually on the verge of being cooked, since its skin was twice as thick, while the surface area was only four times that of an ordinary horse. It was also chronically hungry and had difficulty breathing, since the oesophagus and windpipe were only four times the size of those of an ordinary horse, while the body was eight times as heavy.

This fable was originally told in the late 1970s as a warning against the widespread enthusiasm for genetic manipulation that Bateson already saw as a danger at that time. But it is also generally about complexity and, I would contend, the transformation of quantity into quality.

Another, more directly relevant example is this. In a university department with 50 students, one administrator is sufficient. He or she can serve as secretary, organise exams, keep the budget balanced and give some student advice. When the department gets 100 students, one will not need two, but five administrators. This is because it no longer is possible for one individual mind to possess all necessary knowledge. The department becomes dependent on written routines, registration and forms. The administration no longer knows each individual student and does not know their interests or the level achieved by them, their academic background and so on. So a professional student counsellor has to take care of the relationship with the students. Budget control also becomes so complicated that a financial consultant has to be employed. One also needs a person on the front desk and an IT consultant and finally, in order to keep the staff organised, an office manager.

An organisation can grow for quite a while without changing noticeably. Many enterprises are based on interpersonal relationships, trust and human memory. This works as long as the organisation is small and easily manageable. When the number of employees passes a critical point, the relationships must be formalised and bureaucratised. An example from my part of the world concerns research councils. They award grants and scholarships to the needy (that is, promising researchers, PhD students, brilliant scholars who do not want an academic job, etc.). When there were few applicants, the relationship between the recipient and the council was based on personal trust. It was easy for the research bureaucrats to keep an eye on 'their' scholars; one generally knew what they were up to. As the number of grant recipients has grown, they are increasingly obliged to write regular reports, submit plans for their further work and so on. Thus the research councils have to employ new people to administer the reporting system, at the same time as research fellows spend an increasing amount of time filling in the forms and writing their reports.

This kind of complexification should be familiar from experience of all growing organisations. A further side-effect of growth is the number of meetings that are deemed necessary. Large organisations need many meetings to coordinate their activities; as a result, employees spend an increasing proportion of their working time in meetings coordinating their work instead of doing it.

An example taken from a different field may illustrate how it can be that strictly speaking unproductive meetings tend to fill so much working time. The example is about skyscrapers. Lately, a kind of competition in capitalist machismo has involved people in certain Asian and North American countries, competing over who could build the tallest skyscraper. At the time of writing, Malaysia is leading. The architects have nevertheless noticed a curious problem which may eventually limit the maximum height of tall buildings in the future. It has nothing to do with safety (strangely enough, sky-scrapers do not fall over) or problems for air traffic, but with the number of lifts. A rule of thumb dictates a set of lifts (usually four small or two big ones) for every 15 floors. The taller the building, therefore, the more of the floor area is taken up by lifts. If we follow this line of reasoning to its logical conclusion, it appears that in a 500-floor building, there will be room for nothing but lifts!

It is entirely possible to imagine an organisation which has time for nothing but meetings. (I feel confident that there are depart-ments in ministries that approach this stage.) A solution to the lift problem could be decentralisation. For example, one might partition the building into 100-floor segments. Each set of lifts only runs 100 floors. Then one has to get out and change. Too bad, of course, if one works on the 499th floor, but at least one will then be able to read the paper thoroughly on the way to work. The lower segments will be more crowded than the upper ones; therefore the lower lifts will be very fast, and some of them will be express lifts which do not stop until say, the fiftieth floor.

This kind of solution is identical to the one proposed for organi-sations that waste their employees' time and motivation in exhausting meetings, which force them to do their actual work after office hours. One partitions the enterprise into five parts of the same size, and leaves internal coordination to as few employees as possible.

Since we are still lingering near the ivory towers of academia (which are still so low in most countries that one only has time to skim a tabloid while taking the lift), I will offer another example from there. Like all of the examples in this chapter, it is to do with unintended consequences of uncontrolled growth.

In 1970 there were perhaps a dozen research positions in the then tiny discipline of social anthropology in the Nordic countries. In

1980, the number was at least doubled; in 2000 it was at least ten times the original number. Whenever a new position is established, or an old one becomes vacant, an evaluation committee of three or four persons is appointed. They are obliged to read and evaluate all applications, which – apart from a CV and a brief statement from the applicant – consists of the applicants' most important scientific work. In most cases, this would include an MPhil. dissertation, a PhD thesis and a stack of articles from each applicant; in several cases also a few books. The number of applicants for each position has grown steadily, the amount of writing from each applicant has grown similarly (the pressure to publish has become heavier), and the number of vacancies has grown. A few years ago, I was a member of an evaluation committee for two lecturerships at a small Nordic university. Arriving at the university post office to collect the applications, I realised that I should have brought a wheelbarrow. The parcel weighed in at 32 kilograms (70 pounds). It goes without saying that it is impossible to read everything thoroughly when one is confronted with this kind of quantity. Reading every gram would have taken about a year – the weight of an average sheet is 4.6 grams (assuming 80 gram paper), and much of the material was printed and therefore two-sided, and so the total amount of material for the committee's perusal may have been about 10,000 pages. At the rate of 200 pages a day, reading everything would take two months of solid work. Needless to add, none of us had that kind of continuous time at our disposal then (nor later). The result of this is, truth to tell, that applicants for academic position do not get the thorough treatment they deserve, but also that researchers are obliged to spend weeks ploughing through mountains of material that they will never be able to use in their own research, while the latest journals and books are sitting on the shelf collecting dust.

THERE IS A GROWING AMOUNT OF EVERYTHING

While we are at it: the growth of the number of published books and journals has been staggering during the last years of the twentieth century. In Great Britain, a total of 35,000 books were published in 1975. In 1985, the number had grown to 53,000. Then a leap occurs: during the next decade, the number of books published in the country doubled, to 107,000. The explanation must partly be that new computer technology has made it cheaper and easier to produce books. Writers submit their manuscripts in electronic form, and the page layout is done with a simple and inexpensive programme such as PageMaker or Quark XPress. The first version of PageMaker was shipped at the end of 1986.

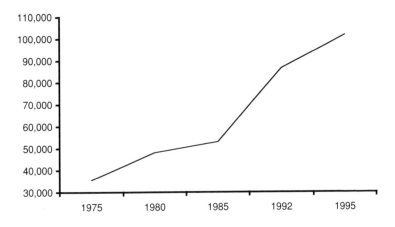

Source: UNESCO

Figure 5.2a Book titles published in the UK, 1975–96

The growth rate for the world as a whole is less spectacular (although the figures are not strictly comparable), but the trend is clear. In 1970, the total number of published books was slightly over half a million. Twenty years later, the number was 842,000. If this trend continues, we have already passed the 1 million mark as I write.

Another indicator is paper consumption. Recall how early prophets of computerisation predicted the advent of the paper-free office, and how the death of the book has been announced regularly for 20 years. Well. The amount of paper used for printing was on a global basis 28 million metric tonnes in 1975. In 2000 it had risen to 97 million tonnes. The woodpulp industry seems to have little to fear from the rise of the Internet and digital television. There is growth in everything to do with information.

It seems likely that a lot of these publications are not primarily produced to be read, even if the literate population in the world has also grown immensely since 1970. Most of the growth in publishing has taken place in the rich countries, where literacy rates have been

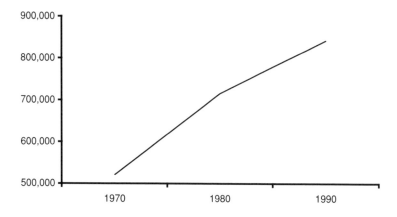

Source: UNESCO

Figure 5.2b Book titles published worldwide, 1970–90

stable and population growth has been slow. We are not talking about the well-stocked libraries of rural Pakistani women here. Regarding academic publications, they are purchased by libraries, sometimes with financial support from the state or a research foundation, and the author depends on being able to place a reasonable number of them on his CV in order to be eligible for a good position. A lot of this material seems to circulate within a

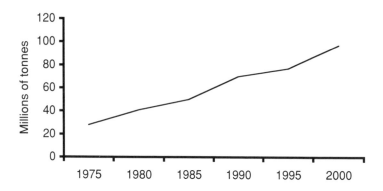

Source: UNESCO

Figure 5.3 Paper consumption in the world, 1975–2000

closed circuit without a real market or readership. Quotation indexes for academic journals indicate that perhaps more than half of all published journal articles in the social sciences are never quoted. One inevitably ventures to ask: are they ever read? It is likely that a sizeable proportion of published academic work is only read by the publisher's editorial consultants, copy-editors and proofreaders, and members of academic evaluation committees. An exaggerated and cynical description? Possibly, but it is not entirely unrealistic.

One of the most perfect exponential growth curves regarding the Internet is, in line with this development, the turnover rate of a company whose main business consists in spreading good old-fashioned, cellulose-based information. The Internet bookshop Amazon.com was launched in July 1995, and during its first fiscal year its turnover was a modest $511,000, which grew to $15,746,000 in the next year. In 1999, the turnover was $1,639,839,000 (more than one and a half billion dollars), and most of this was still book sales. And the growth rate continues to be astonishing: between the second quarter of 1999 and the second quarter of 2000, the turnover grew by 84 per cent!

Publishing which swears by wood pulp is, in other words, alive and kicking, although 'everybody' talks of the Internet or something

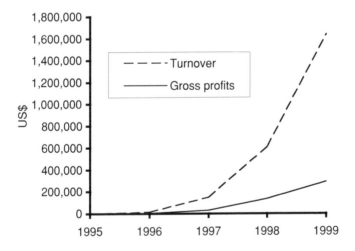

Source: www.amazon.com

Figure 5.4 Amazon.com. 1995–99

like it as the main source of information in the near future. Similarly, there is little to indicate that people talk less on the telephone since the introduction of e-mail and fax. The growth rate of telephony has been phenomenal over the last 15 years. Two of the most important telephone routes in the world are the clusters of lines that cross the Atlantic and the Pacific oceans, generally channelling calls to and from the USA. It has been technically possible to make transatlantic calls since 1927, but as late as the 1970s, it was cumbersome and expensive to place a long-distance call from, say, Gothenburg to relatives in Seattle. When I did my first ethnographic fieldwork in Mauritius in 1986, I had to make my way physically to the national Telecom centre in the capital, whenever I felt the need to reassure my mother that I was still alive. I had to take an old, smelly bus to town, walk five blocks in the dazing heat, stand in a queue to order the call, wait for my turn, walk into a closet and talk over a poor connection with echo and noise, while my diminishing wad of rupees was depleted at frightening speed. I also spent the autumn of 1999 in Mauritius, and apart from the fact that I could call home from any telephone, I found myself one day in the shadow of a mango tree near the sea, far from the nearest town, making an inexpensive, crystal clear call to Oslo.

Between 1986 and 1996, the number of telephone lines across the Atlantic increased from 100,000 to 1,974,000, that is a growth of nearly 2,000 per cent. The corresponding figures for the Pacific were 41,000 in 1986 and 1,098,600 in 1996. In 1985, the total use of telecommunications in the world (telephony, fax, data transmission) added up to 15 billion minutes. Ten years later, the number was quadrupled to 60 billion minutes. The figure for 2000 is estimated at 95 billion minutes. Few traditional industries can match this growth rate.

The suppliers of these services are prepared for exponential growth in the near future, extrapolating from current trends. In the first five years of the twenty-first century, there are plans to send out no less than 1,000 new satellites dedicated to telecommunications. The main tendency is for this kind of communication to become increasingly mobile, wireless, disembedded from place. One can increasingly send and receive information anywhere, anytime. We have still seen only the beginning, but it points in a particular direction. Mobile phones replace stationary phones, PDAs (Personal Digital Assistants, i.e. handheld computers) replace notebooks, filofaxes and address books, and are already able to connect to the

Internet; people have ISDN connections installed in their remote wood cabins and are given laptops by their employers.

In 1990, mobile phones were still a sort of gadget associated with particular professions – taxi drivers, travelling salesmen and perhaps a few others. This generation of mobile phones were powered by the lighter socket in the car and a box that filled half the trunk. At the end of 2000, altogether 3 million mobile phone subscriptions have been sold in Norway (a country with a population of 4.5 million). In Finland, the home of Nokia (ten years ago the home of... well, vodka and wood pulp), children on average possess more than one mobile phone each.

Since wireless communication grows so fast, one might perhaps believe that it would replace the other, traditional form of communication, embodied in technology such as cars and planes. Many of those who see the Internet as an environmentally sound alternative to travelling, have been hoping for this to happen (just as some predicted, around 1980, the coming of the paper-free office). So far, nothing indicates that this is about to happen. On the contrary, we seem to get more of everything. Both road and air traffic grow surprisingly fast globally.

In the 1990s, air traffic grew at a rate of between 5 and 7 per cent a year. In the spring of 2000, the international air traffic association,

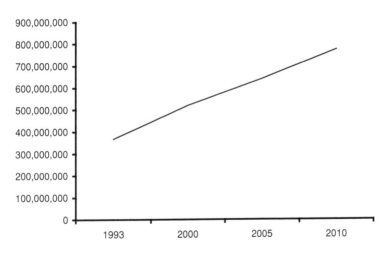

Source: Air Transport Action Group (www.atag.org)

Figure 5.5a Number of air passengers in Europe, 1993–2010

IATA, estimated that the total number of travellers would grow from 1.6 billion to 2.3 billion between 1999 and 2010. IATA also predicts that the number of passengers arriving in the USA by plane will grow from 79 million (1993) via 121 million (2000) to 226 million in 2010. This growth curve will soon make it difficult to avoid a nearly perfect vertical line when it is transferred to graph paper. And, if these figures sound large, it must be kept in mind that they refer exclusively to travellers to and from the USA; air travel within that country is not included. Regarding Europe, total air traffic is predicted to double in 15 years from 2000. The total number of passenger kilometres, incidentally, is estimated to increase by 50 per cent from 1994 to 2001.

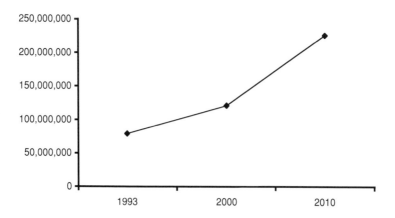

Source: IATA

Figure 5.5b Air passengers to and from the USA, 1993–2010

For the time being, three issues are discussed particularly intensively by those international organisations that are responsible for civilian air traffic: the lack of vacant radio frequencies (a result of both more planes and more mobile phones), delays and airport architecture – how do you design an airport which can easily double its capacity in a few years without compromising passenger services and security? If one travels regularly via busy airports, in other words, one might as well get used to being on a permanent construction site.

This is not science fiction. The researchers who reached these figures have simply extrapolated from the trends of the last decades. As is the case with other exponential growth curves, the rate of growth is relatively stable, but the figures are becoming incomprehensibly large.

Until the late 1970s, air travel was in general an exclusive, expensive way of travelling. It has been democratised, just like remote calls on the telephone net. In 1960, a 3-minute call from London to New York cost the equivalent of $240 (in 1990 dollars). In 2000, the price was $2 (in 1990 dollars). Air travel has become similarly inexpensive, and nowhere is this more evident than in the economic sector which is, perhaps, the third largest in the world (following weapons and drugs), namely tourism. According to that other organisation called the WTO, the World Tourism Organization, tourism accounts for about 12 per cent of the world economy. The WTO further estimates the total turnover in the tourism industry in 2001 to $3.5 trillion dollars (a trillion is a thousand billions, one followed by twelve zeros.) The number of tourists has grown by a factor of 20 since 1950.

In 2020, an estimated 1.6 billion persons will travel abroad. The Mediterranean area, still the most popular foreign destination for North Europeans, received 100,000 tourists annually in 1955. In

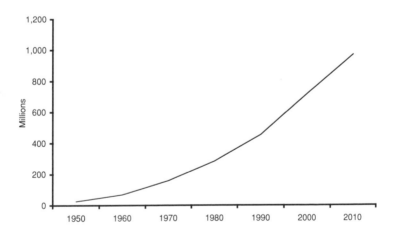

Source: World Tourist Organization

Figure 5.6 Number of tourists in the world, 1950–2010

1970, the number was 2 million, and in 1990 6.5 million. The development continues. If, in other words, one travels from Gatwick to the Costa del Sol as a tourist, one moves from one permanent construction site to another.

These figures are dizzying. The growth curves point almost straight upwards. At a more encompassing level, it may be noted that the total flow of capital in the world is estimated to have grown by a factor of 100 since 1975; it has increased, in other words, by 1,000 per cent in 25 years. This figure proves more than anything that however fashionable it may be to talk about globalisation, it does refer to a very tangible and consequential reality.

THE GROWTH RATES IN CYBERSPACE SURPASS EVERYTHING ELSE

Still, I have hardly mentioned the Internet in this chapter. The most spectacular examples of exponential growth in our time are those that relate directly to electronic information technology, and the most obvious examples concern the entry of computers into the everyday life of the world and the appearance of the Internet as a serious competitor to other channels for transmitting information, from newspapers to television. The changes have come about fast. It took the radio 38 years from its invention until it reached 50 million people. In the case of television, some decades later, the same figure was reached in 13 years. With the World Wide Web, it took four years. Is anybody still in doubt as to whether change accelerated during the twentieth century?

An inevitable example of exponential growth in the computer world is the development of Microsoft from the foundation of the firm in 1975 up to the present. During its first year in business, the company generated $16,000 in surplus. Its growth from that year onwards has followed the same logic as the number of grains of wheat accorded to the mythical inventor of chess. The surplus could for a long time be doubled at each crossroads without making Bill Gates and his companions rich. Towards the end of the 1980s, the direction of the growth curve began to shift, seen from the vantage-point of the late 1990s. The rate of growth was roughly constant, but the numbers were now so large that a doubling of the surplus entailed rather a lot of money going into the pockets of the shareholders. Figure 5.8 shows this clearly.

Microsoft has never been particularly innovative technologically, but the company has been incredibly skilful at conquering new markets. One market that they nevertheless do not dominate is the important server market. A server is a box which stores, organises, sends and receives information on the Internet. All information on the Net passes via one or several servers, whether it is e-mail, WWW pages, chat messages or something else. The leading company in this sector, both on the hardware and software side, is Cisco. In five years – from 1995 to 1999 – their turnover grew from $2.2 billion (which is already a sizeable sum) to $12.2 billion. The profits grew accordingly.

The number of hosts (web sites) on the WWW grew from 3 million in July 1994 to 72 million in January 2000. The outlook for people seeking to make money from the web is also reasonable, in spite of several temporary backlashes in the last few years. The estimated figure in this respect goes from nearly nothing to $377 million in 2000, and is expected to pass the $1,200 million mark in 2002. If anyone doubts the optimism of this estimate, think of Microsoft, Cisco and the Emperor's grain stores!

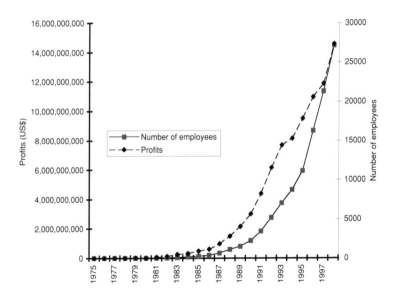

Source: www.microsoft.com

Figure 5.7 Microsoft, 1975–98

Information in electronic form has an interesting quality distinguishing it from both paper-based information and all other physical objects. It is not reduced in quantity when one gives it away. If, say, I charge my Visa card with $249 (virtual money; it exists only in cyberspace) to download the latest version of my preferred web design software from a server in the USA, the stocks of the supplier are not reduced by as much as a gram. One possesses information, one sells it, and one has as much left. A supplier of information has stores which can in principle never be emptied. If I give a lecture about Darwinism for a few hundred students in the social sciences (which I do a couple of times a year), I do not have any less knowledge about Darwin afterwards. (Quite the contrary, as a matter of fact!) The worst thing that could happen to a supplier of bits, bytes and ideas, is that it becomes outmoded – and the probability of this happening increases year by year. This quality of electronic (and spoken) information as a commodity, makes it particularly promising as a candidate for exponential growth curves. So far, few have regarded the growth in information as a problem on a par with population growth or growth in industrial pollution. It may be high time that we do.

This is not merely a personal lament from a scholar who has had his fill of unfiltered information. Exponential growth in informa-

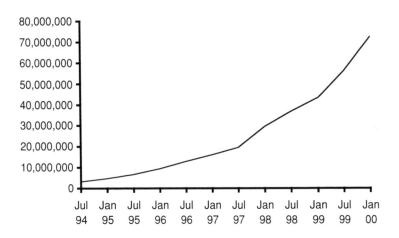

Source: Internet Software Consortium (www.isc.org)

Figure 5.8 Number of WWW hosts in the world, 1994–2000

tion functions in roughly the same way everywhere. Information is partitioned into little pieces, it finds paths to reach the last vacant cubic centimetre in the brain of the reader. Even readers/watchers/listeners who do not spend half their day or more consuming ready-made bits of information are affected by this. Perhaps they fill the tank of their car at a petrol station where the nozzle of the petrol hose is now decorated with an advertisement; perhaps they are addicted to SMS messages; or perhaps they simply spend their evenings trying to relax in front of the television, which is a medium of accelerating speed. Even if one watches just one news programme a day, or for that matter a week, and protects oneself against other sources of information, that particular programme does not become any slower for that reason.

TIME GOES TOWARDS ZERO

Most of the examples presented in this chapter belong to the most common kind of exponential curve – that is, the case of the bacterial colony, but not the chessboard and the grains of wheat. They are curves where the x axis represents duration. When the curve makes its steep movement upwards on the right-hand side, an implication is that more events are squeezed into the time span in question. They

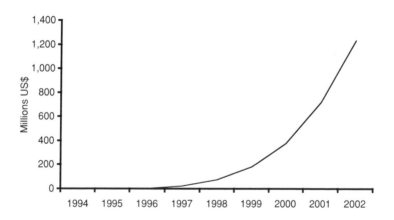

Source: www.nua.ie, 2000

Figure 5.9 Surplus generated by the Internet, 1996–2002

illustrate, in other words, the compression of time: more and more information, consumption, movement and activity is being pushed into the available time, which is relatively constant (although there exist lunatics who earnestly try to 'sleep more efficiently'). When the line is perfectly vertical, time has ceased to exist. This, naturally, is an extreme case which is difficult to imagine in practice; it is a state which occurs only when the news is outdated the moment it comes on the air, when fashion clothes are *passé* just as they hit the shops and so on.

As this chapter has shown, growth curves with exponential tendencies can be plotted on to many, apparently unrelated phenomena in our time. Many of them are admittedly caused by the spreading of information technology, but not all. Global population growth continues to look quite exponential, although it is currently about to flatten out. Besides, the world's population doubles less quickly than, say, the number of tourists, the number of web sites or the number of literate persons in the world. Briefly put, the number of readers and writers, the number of tourists and users of Microsoft Windows, the numbers of books published and mobile phones grow much more rapidly than the world's population. The same could be said about the number of cafés and Indian restaurants in Oslo during the past ten years, global flows of capital and the world's total air traffic. There is a connection between these growth trends, even if it is not self-evident. When the population grows somewhere (in a village, a country or on a planet), space becomes more scarce. This does not imply that ceiling levels are necessarily reduced or that people will have to go to bed hungry, but that complexity grows. When growing numbers read and write, go to school, send e-mail, travel by bus, train or aeroplane, the networks that connect people become more dense. Attractive plots of land are sought after ever more intensively, and scarcity increases with growing density – property is much, much more expensive in central London than in the Hebrides – and a kind of property which is particularly scarce, is any vacant moment in people's lives.

It goes without saying that exponential growth is eventually bound to alter its course. Sooner or later. The question is, what is sooner and what is later? A flattening of growth curves happened in the case of the Ebola virus in the 1990s, it will happen with AIDS; it has happened to world population growth, and it will happen with the disappearance of the rainforests; it has recently happened to annual computer sales in Scandinavia, and it will happen to Microsoft. Just how and when this change of direction will come about, is impossible to say. In the case of the rainforests, it will occur when there is no more rainforest left, but not necessarily any earlier. However, as the chess example indicates, the growth curve points upwards quite steeply even if we just isolate the first ten or twenty squares, long before the entire world's production of wheat is implied. If one had studied the development of Microsoft during its first ten years, from 1975 to 1985, one would already have been able to plot a pretty steep growth curve. Perhaps in 2030, analysts will say that air passenger traffic was still modest in 2000, but after 2010, the figures became increasingly intolerable. It may well be the case that the number of telephone connections across the Pacific, the number of passenger kilometres travelled by plane and the number of web sites will continue to grow exponentially for a while yet, without a critical mass of people seeing it as a disaster. But the price of this growth is already evident – it will not necessarily be environmental degradation in the traditional sense, but the fact that time approaches zero. More and more is squeezed into every free moment, and the gaps are filled. The result of this compression I now propose to discuss in terms of *stacking*.

6   Stacking

'This is just so, I mean, like, *last week*!'
(Comment on jeans ad, heard on Oslo tram)

The first real American soap opera to hit the Scandinavian markets was *Dynasty*. It was introduced to a curious and excited audience in the same year as multi-channel viewing appeared in the same countries, thanks to satellite and cable transmissions, namely 1983. Like many thousands of others, my friends and I went into the kitchen and turned on our old black-and-white television on the first evening of *Dynasty*, to find out what this was. After a few weeks we believed we had understood it, and ceased watching the programme since we had other things to do (chiefly wearing black clothes and staring blankly in front of us in grim concert venues that had been redecorated to look like abandoned factories). The years went by. Six years later, I travelled to tropical Trinidad in the Caribbean Sea to carry out ethnographic fieldwork. In Trinidad, it turned out, a large part of the population followed *Dynasty* (although other soap operas, particularly the lunchtime show *The Young and the Restless*, were even more popular). I rented a TV set and began to watch *Dynasty* again, since a golden rule of anthropology admonishes practitioners doing fieldwork to try to do whatever it is that the natives do.

I had been absent from the series for six years, and it took me about 30 seconds to get into the narrative again. Like other programmes of the same kind, *Dynasty* was tailored for the multi-channel format. It was being produced in the awareness that the viewers would restlessly finger their remote control while watching, ready to switch channels at the first indication of inertia. It presupposed commercial breaks every seventh minute or so, and so the cliffhangers were overdone and frequent. The cost of this breathless, fast kind of drama is a lack of progression. Like other serials of the same kind, *Dynasty* was a drama which stood still at enormous speed.

THE MOMENT PRECLUDES DEVELOPMENT

As late as the 1970s, most European countries had one, two or a maximum of three national television channels. Many were state-

run and free of commercials. Until the early to mid-1970s, programming in black and white dominated the offering in many
countries. One of the most popular drama series at the time was *The
Ashton Family*, based on John Finch's novel. This series, which was
a deadly serious narrative about an English family during the
Second World War, was typically *slow* and *cumulative*. If one had
missed just one episode, one lost the narrative thread, since the
people and their relationships changed as the story unfolded. It presupposed loyal, patient viewers without a lot of noisy alternatives.
In this way, the series could be based on a rhythm where particular
events slowly reverberated through the cast, leaving their imprint
on the future direction of the action. While *Dynasty* was based on
the explosive moment, *The Ashton Family* was based on linear time
and organic growth.

This example was not chosen because it in itself is particularly
interesting, but because it illustrates a fundamental change in our
culture; from the relatively slow and linear to the fast and
momentary. Television has, over the past couple of decades, become
an ever faster medium, and the same change has taken place in
radio, which generally seems to become more hectic and breathless
the more channels one has to choose between. The relationship
between the two TV series, further, is analogous to the relationship
between the World Wide Web and the book. The book is *sequential*:
you begin with page 1 and read it in a particular order. The writer
controls the drift of the reading, and is therefore at liberty to
construct a cumulative, linear plot or argument. The reader reaches
ever new plateaux of knowledge or insight as she (most readers are
women) moves through the text. This, at any rate, is an ideal
depiction of the art of reading.

There are several crucial differences between the web and a library
of paper publications. Above all, information on the web is not
organised, be it alphabetically or in any other way. Different themes
and pages are linked together in partly random ways. The web is not
hierarchical either, the millions of sites in existence are all accessible
at the same level.

Active users of the WWW have for years felt that it is a dense and
cumbersome jungle which grows a little darker and denser every day.
When one surfs the web in search of information which seems not
to be there (despite 100,000 hits on Alta Vista), it is tempting to
conclude that the web is a real-world incarnation of Jorge Luis
Borges's philosophical fable about the library of Babel. This mythical

library contained, apart from all books that had been written, all the books that *could have been written* – that is, every possible combination of the letters of the alphabet. Everything is available out there, but everything else is also available out there, and like almost everywhere else, Murphy's Law operates on the web as well: under normal circumstances, one will find *everything else* first. As a media researcher expressed it: the Internet is like the large oceans. They are full of gold, but it costs a fortune to exploit even a tiny fraction of it. The web is uncensored, democratic and chaotic. Everything is already stacked on top of everything else there, but it still grows a little every day.

FILTERS AGAINST FRAGMENTATION DO NOT REMOVE FRAGMENTATION

The most important tool needed to navigate on the web is neither a superfast computer with lots of RAM, nor a broadband connection or the latest news in web browsers (although all of this helps), but good filters. As mentioned several times already, there is no scarcity of information in information society. There is far too much of it. With no opportunity to filter away that available information which one does not need, one is lost and will literally drown in zeros and ones.

Many are willing to help web users to find their way, not least because it can pay off. Several of the greatest economic successes in cyberspace are companies which have specialised in web searches. The first one was Yahoo!, and currently the largest one is Alta Vista. It is sometimes said that the homes of these search engines are the only web pages that can rival the major pornographic sites for popularity. In their simplest form, they function as digital indexes. If, for example, you want to map out the movements of saxophonist Didier Malherbe during the last few months, or you want to read about the current political developments in Kosovo or the latest operating system from Apple, you type the keywords, and in a matter of seconds you get a list of links to relevant web sites, normally a useless list containing thousands of links. Then you narrow the search to include, say, '+Apple +OSX +download', and soon you will have a manageable list of less than a hundred hits. You have reduced the universe to that microscopic segment you are interested in.

Searching with Alta Vista or a similar engine is not much more advanced than searching a digital phone book. However, new methods for filtering information are continuously being developed, whether the aim is to help frustrated web surfers to protect themselves against unwanted information, or to sell them goods. The methods used in the latter instance are often inventive and seductive. For a few years, I have been greeted by www.amazon.com in the following way – like millions of other customers: 'Hello Thomas! We have recommendations for you!', followed by a few 'hot titles' in the subject areas that fall within my fields of interest, according to Amazon's software. Often, however, filters are less than functional. If you feel the world is not chaotic enough, I recommend an evening of reading with Yahoo's categories as a point of departure.

In the old days, most of us tended to accept the information we were offered, whether it was the daily newspaper or the radio news. Today, the freedom of choice is unlimited. Via the web, one can listen to Midwestern C&W channels, subscribe to specialised news services – say, one can refuse to take in sad news about war and violence, one can follow Malaysian weather or the Harare stock exchange daily, or one can read everything about the latest offerings from Hollywood and nothing else. These kinds of tailored services are available from several sources and in several formats (e-mail, web, WAP). At Microsoft News, one may choose one's personal categories from business and health to weather, sports and travel; while America Online has web centres with material on everything from cars to research and local news. Other kinds of services include UnCover Real, which offers to e-mail you the table of contents of your favourite journals regularly.

I have already indicated, in the previous chapter, why there is a pressing need for this kind of filtering; it is also evident that if these kinds of filters (and greatly improved versions of them) become sufficiently widespread, there is eventually little left of the national public spheres. There is then no guarantee that the neighbour has heard about the government's latest budget cuts or the latest plane crash. It may even be that he was so busy following software developments at Apple that he is blissfully unaware of the perpetually tragic state of the national English football team. Unlike the good old media (such as newspapers and nationwide television channels), news on the web is placeless and without clear priorities. Everything is in principle just as important as everything else, and besides, distance is bracketed, which entails that it is no more difficult to access the electronic edition of the *Hindu* than the corresponding edition of the *Independent*.

Since everything is available on the Web and there exist no fixed, socially shared routines for distinguishing between wanted and unwanted information, each individual is forced to develop their own paths, creating their own, personal cuts of the world. (In software marketing jargon, this is called *customisation*.)

A telling image of the direction current developments are taking, is the currently popular system for digital storage of music, MP3 (which may have been replaced by MP4 by the time this is being read). Still, most people buy music on CDs, which are a direct extension of the old vinyl LP. Like a printed book or newspaper, a CD is a finished, completed product with a beginning, a middle and an end. One cannot cut and paste the content according to whim; even if one is mighty sick of the overexposed first movement in Beethoven's fifth symphony, one cannot replace it by an overture from one of Wagner's operas. One may like it or not, but that is how it is.

MP3 is a file format for electronic transmission of music. There are both virtual players (for use on the computer) and physical players of the Walkman kind available, and there are enormous amounts of music on the web, which anyone can download. Following several lawsuits (the most famous of which involved the successful Napster site), it is likely that people will increasingly have to pay for their music downloads, which so far have been largely free (and legally ambiguous, to say the least). When one buys Beethoven's fifth, one thus pays for a password which allows a single download of the entire symphony. When one then has the symphony in MP3 format, one can finally evade that tiring first movement, or for that matter the sluggish second movement; one may edit the work just as one wants. Unlike a completed CD, an MP3 playlist contains only pieces which the listener has actively chosen, such as – say – a tune by Oasis, the second movement of Mahler's fourth, the first movement of Bártok's second string quartet, two Beatles classics and an old recording of Miles Davis and John Coltrane. Then one may copy the entire thing on to a portable MP3 player for use in the car or on the tube.

MP3 is a concrete example of the logic of the web. In principle, everything is available out there, and each individual user puts together his or her own, personal totality out of the fragments. MP3 relates to the CD as the web relates to the book. The Internet fits perfectly with, and is also in at least two ways an important contributing cause of the prevailing neo-liberal ideology. WWW (and multi-channel television, and MP3, and 'flexible work'...) offers freedom and choice by the bucket-load. On the deficit side of the balance, we have to note, among other things, 'internal cohesion, meaningful context and slowness'.

PIECES REPLACE TOTALITIES

We are slowly moving towards the main point of this chapter, and as a prelude, I shall add yet another facet to the description of the Internet. The literary theorist Marshall McLuhan (1915–80), who rose to fame as a media theorist in the 1960s, once wrote about the difference between a *haptic* and an *optic* culture, a contrast that refers to varying usage of the senses under different regimes of information technology. Pre-modern people lived, according to McLuhan, in a 'haptic harmony' – all senses were equal and functioned as a totality, a unity. The 'auditive-tactile' senses (hearing and touch) were essential both for experience and for knowledge. With literacy, the visual sense gained the upper hand and suppressed the others. (In Plato, this has already come about; just think about his cave allegory!) Humans thus became increasingly inhibited and narrow-minded. Writing gave us 'an eye for an ear', and to McLuhan, this entails something of a fall from grace. To him, the pure, linear text is a fragmenting and reductive medium which removes the reader from a total experience with the full use of all his or her senses. In television, McLuhan saw an opportunity to re-create that sensory unity which the advent of writing had destroyed, and he had a great – some would say incomprehensible – optimism on behalf of this new medium when he wrote his most important books in the 1960s.

A decade and a half after his death, McLuhan was launched, by the magazine *WIRED*, as a patron saint for the Internet. Much of what he said in general about new media (especially television) fits the World Wide Web surprisingly well. I agree with the main thrust of McLuhan's argument, but my conclusion is the exact opposite of his. It is not the book, but television that functions in a fragmenting way. The book relates to the WWW as single-channel television relates to multi-channel television, and linear time is a valuable resource that we cannot afford to waste. In this context, it is tempting to propose a whole series of contrasts that may illustrate the transition from industrial to informational society, from nation-building to globalisation, from book to monitor. We may, for example, depict the changes like this:

Industrial society	*Informational society*
CD/vinyl record	MP3
Book	WWW
Single-channel TV	Multi-channel TV
Letter	E-mail
Stationary telephone	Mobile telephone

... and while we are at it, why not also:

Lifelong monogamy	Serial monogamy
The era of the gold watch	The era of flexible work
Depth	Breadth
Linear time	Fragmented contemporariness
Scarcity of information	Scarcity of freedom from information

More about these last points in the final chapters. For now, I shall concentrate on one effect of the new informational regime, and I will give McLuhan my support on a crucial point: the tidal waves of information fragments typical of our kind of society stimulate a style of thought that is less reminiscent of the strict, logical, linear thinking characteristic of industrial society than of the freely associating, poetical, metaphorical thinking that characterised many non-modern societies. Instead of ordering knowledge in tidy rows, information society offers cascades of decontextualised signs more or less randomly connected to each other.

The cause of this change is neither the introduction of the World Wide Web nor multi-channel television as such. It is instead the fact, documented in the previous chapter, that there is rapid growth in every area to do with information, but no more time than formerly available to digest it.

CONTEMPORARY CULTURE RUNS AT FULL SPEED WITHOUT MOVING AN INCH

Put differently: the close cousins of acceleration and exponential growth lead to *vertical stacking*. Since the flanks are reserved for small groups with special interests (e.g. progressive rock, theoretical physics, veteran buses, social anthropological method, Greek poetry), more and more is stacked up in the middle. Translated from the spatial metaphor to the temporal dimension, this means that since there is no vacant time to spread information in, it is compressed and stacked in time spans that become shorter and shorter. High-rise buildings appear in the centre, sprawling bungalows in the suburbs. The logic that characterises *Dynasty* and similar multi-channel, commercial-financed television series, is the same as that which entails that the most competitive news programmes are shorter than the others, that commercials become shorter and shorter – and, yes, I shall offer more examples eventually.

The concept of vertical stacking is taken from a book which – of all things – deals with progressive rock, a musical genre that was particularly popular among long-haired and great-coated boys and men in the first half of the 1970s, and which was forced more or less underground when punk not only made the dominant youth culture jeer dismissively at anyone daring to go on stage with stacks of synthesizers, but which also made it a virtue not to be able to play an instrument properly. Like everything else, progressive rock was re-awakened by Internet-based retro waves in the second half of the 1990s – sometimes, it must be conceded, with disastrous results. The North American philosophy professor Bill Martin has tried, in his broad defence plea for bands he loves (from Yes to King Crimson), to explain what, to his mind, is wrong with the computer- and studio-based dance music of the last decade, including house, techno, drum'n'bass and other genres which have little in common apart from the fact that they can be described as varieties of non-linear, repetitive, rhythmical dance music. This is music which in his view lacks progression and direction, which – unlike, say, Beethoven, Miles Davis and Led Zeppelin – is not heading anywhere. Enjoyment of such music is generally undertaken by entering a room full of sound where a great number of aural things are happening, and staying there until it no longer feels cool. Martin's preferred music is linear and has an inner development – although it may often be partly improvised. About the new rhythmic music, he has this to say:

> As with postmodern architecture, the idea in this stacking is that, in principle, any sound can go with any other sound. Just as, however, even the most eclectic pastiche of a building must all the same have some sort of foundation that anchors it to the

ground, vertically stacked music often depends on an insisting beat. There are layers of trance stacked on top of dance, often without much in the way of stylistic integration.

Martin doubts that this music will be capable of creating anything really new. 'The vertical-stacking approach implicitly (or even explicitly) accepts the idea that music (or art more generally) is now simply a matter of trying out the combinations, filling out the grid.' I will not risk my personal friendships with trance adepts by supporting this argument, but instead draw attention to the fact that, inadvertently, Martin offers an excellent description of an aspect of the tyranny of the moment: there are layers upon layers on top of each other, every vacant spot is filled, and there is little by way of internal integration.

STACKING REPLACES INTERNAL DEVELOPMENT

The exceptionally gifted musician and composer Brian Eno is both godfather and pioneer in much of the new rhythmic music. Already in the 1970s, he developed his concept 'Ambient Music', non-linear music which could function as an aural wallpaper, but which was also intended to be 'as listenable as it was ignorable', as the liner notes of *Music for Airports* put it.

Few know the field of rhythmic music better than Eno. In 1995 he kept a diary, and published (presumably an edited version of) it the following year. On 8 September, he made a sketch of the 'phases' of popular music since the breakthrough of rock'n'roll. He proposes ten phases plus an eleventh one, which he locates to the near future. What is interesting in our context is Eno's category number 10, that is the period 1991–95, up to the time of writing. While the other eras have labels such as 'synth pop, 4th world' or 'Glam', he characterises the 1990s like this: 'See '64–'68, add '76–'78'. In other words nothing new, but re-hashes of former trends. As a moderately interested bystander, my distinct impression tends to confirm Eno's view: for several years now, we seem to have everything at once. Every imaginable retro trend exists, at the same time as the big names of bygone eras remain big today, or – as in the case of the Welsh crooner Tom Jones – are being re-awakened by nostalgics. Apart from non-linear, repetitive dance music, the 1990s saw major breakthroughs of pop groups that sounded roughly like The Beatles, heavy metal groups that took up the challenge where Purple and Zeppelin left it in the mid-1970s, 'neo-psychedelic' bands that sound somewhat like the Soft Machine of 1968 or the Pink Floyd of 1965 – and at the same time, the really big names remain artists like Dylan, the Stones and Santana, who have been around for nearly 40 years.

Just as progressive politics is fuelled by a linear faith in progress – a strong, moral idea of development – progressive rock (and many other kinds of music) had an inbuilt faith in progress. The musicians wanted to take their kind of music to new heights, break with the past, create something new and better. Martin discusses the difference between this concept and the new non-linear music as an instance of the modern/postmodern contrast, which is unfortunate, as modernist contemporary music has been non-linear for nearly a hundred years.

Anyway, there are two general points emerging from this idiosyncratic (and far from representative) discussion of trends in popular music that may be linked directly to the issues at hand.

First, stacking of trends implies that there is no change, but mere recirculation. Rock and pop may be surface phenomena, but they are also barometers. When Beatles clones like Oasis, geriatric groups like the Stones and chubby crooners of the generic Phil Collins type (who would have believed, in 1975, that this man – who at his best played the drums like an octopus on speed – would turn into Elton John?) are the undisputed masters of the field, this may be symptomatic of a culture unable to renew itself. As Martin expresses it: there is no real creativity, but a continuous stream of new combinations. I shall return to this in the final chapter, to argue that the filling of gaps typical of the tyranny of the moment is seriously detrimental to creativity. The new arises unexpectedly from the gaps created by slack in time budgets, not from crowded schedules.

Second, the listener's situation is radically different between rock/jazz and the new rhythmic music. The latter goes on and on; the former has a beginning, a long middle (internal development) and an end or climax. Interestingly, Indonesian gamelan music has been a significant source of inspiration to many of those who work with repetitive music, among them the minimalist composer Steve Reich. This is music developed in a traditional, ritualistic culture with no linear concept of development. The link with gamelan music is far from uninteresting, considering McLuhan's (and my) view to the effect that an essentially non-linear way of being in time is being strengthened in contemporary culture.

To readers whose relationship to gamelan music, minimalism, trip-hop and progressive rock is loose, or perhaps even one of indifference, this discussion may seem a bit esoteric. But there is more to say about the matter before we leave it entirely. Somewhere in his enormous work about the information age, Manuel Castells has chosen to include a paragraph about new age music. He regards it as the classical music of our era (a debatable assertion, but all right), and describes it as an expression for 'the double reference to moment and eternity; me and the universe, the self and the net'. Desert winds and ocean waves create the backdrop for many of the repetitive patterns that make up new age music. It is a droning, time-less and lingering kind of music; an antidote to the quotidian rat-race, but also perfectly symmetrical to it, since it brackets the passage of time.

Put differently: when growing amounts of information are distributed at growing speed, it becomes increasingly difficult to create narratives, orders, developmental sequences. The fragments threaten to become hegemonic. This has consequences for the ways we relate to knowledge, work and lifestyle in a wide sense. Cause and effect, internal organic growth, maturity and experience; such categories are under heavy pressure in this situation. The examples from music, which are clearly debatable (many of us are passionate in this area, aren't we?), are chiefly meant as illustrations. The phenomenon as such is naturally much more widespread, and journalism, education, work, politics and domestic life, just to mention a few areas, are affected by vertical stacking. Let us take a look at journalism first.

THE LAW OF DIMINISHING RETURNS STRIKES WITH A VENGEANCE

In a profoundly pessimistic and critical pamphlet about the misery of television, Pierre Bourdieu develops a familiar, but far from unimportant argument. He claims that the fragmented temporality of television, with its swift transitions and fast-paced journalism, creates an intellectual public culture which favours a particular kind of participant. Bourdieu speaks of them as *fast-thinkers*. Whereas the Belgian cartoon hero Lucky Luke is famous for drawing his gun faster than his own shadow, fast-thinkers are described as 'thinkers who think faster than an accelerating bullet'. They are the people who are able, in a couple of minutes of direct transmission, to explain what is wrong with the economic policies of the EU, why one ought to read Kant's *Critique of Pure Reason* this summer, or explain the origins of racist pseudo-science. It is nonetheless a fact that some of the sharpest minds need time to reflect and more time (much more, in some cases) to make an accurate, sufficiently nuanced statement on a particular issue. This kind of thinker becomes invisible and virtually deprived of influence, according to Bourdieu, in this rushed era. (In a banal sense, Bourdieu is obviously wrong. No contemporary thinker is more influential than Bourdieu himself, and obviously he does not define himself as a fast-thinker.)

Bourdieu's argument is congruent with the observation that media appeal has become the most important capital of politicians – not, in other words, their political message or cohesive vision. This is not an entirely new phenomenon; in the USA, the first indication of this development came with John F. Kennedy's victory over Richard M. Nixon. Anyway, a result, in Bourdieu's view, is that the people who speak like machine-guns, in boldface and capital letters, who are given airtime and influence – not the slow and systematic ones.

What is wrong with this? Why should people who have the gift of being able to think fast and accurately, be stigmatised in this way? In a word, what is wrong about thinking fast? Nothing in particular, apart from the fact that some thoughts only function in a slow mode, and that some lines of reasoning can only be developed in a continuous fashion, without the interruptions of an impatient journalist who wants to 'move on' (where?) in the programme. Bourdieu mentions an example many academics will be able to identify with. A few years ago, Bourdieu published *The State Nobility*, a study of symbolic power and elite formation in the French education system. Bourdieu had been actively interested in the field for twenty years, and the book had been long in the making. A journalist proposed a debate between Bourdieu and the president of the alumni organisation of *les grandes Écoles*; the latter would speak 'for' and Bourdieu would speak 'against'. 'And', he sums up sourly: 'he hadn't a clue as to why I refused.'

A topic Bourdieu does not treat explicitly, but which is an evident corollary of his views, is the diminishing returns of media participation following the information explosion. If, before the 1990s, one was invited to contribute to a radio or television programme, one appeared well-prepared in the studio. One might shave (even if the medium was radio!), make certain to wear a freshly ironed shirt and a proper tie, and go into the studio in a slightly nervous state determined to make one's points clearly and concisely. Nowadays, an increasing number of people in the know do not even bother to take part in radio or television transmissions, and if they do, their contributions frequently tend towards the half-hearted and lukewarm. As both viewers and guests on TV shows are aware, each programme has a diminishing impact as the number of channels grow, and the greater the number of channels and talkshows, the less impact each of them has. It is almost as if Andy Warhol was deliberately understating his point when, directly influenced by McLuhan, he said that in 'the future', everybody would be famous for 15 minutes. (Today, he might have said seconds.)

A related effect of stacking and acceleration in the media world, is the tendency for news to become shorter and shorter. A tired joke about the competition for attention among tabloids, consists in the remark that when war eventually breaks out for real, the papers will only have space for the 'W' on the front page. The joke illustrates the principle of diminishing returns (or falling marginal value). In basic economics courses, teachers tend to use food and drink as examples to explain this principle, which is invaluable in an accelerating culture: if you are thirsty, the first soda has very high value for you. The second one is also quite valuable, and you may even – if your thirst is considerable – be willing to pay for the third one. But then, the many soda cans left in the shop suddenly have no value at all to you; you are unwilling to pay a penny for any of them. Tender steaks, further, are highly valuable if you are only allowed to savour them once a month; when steak becomes daily fare, its value decreases dramatically. The marginal value of a commodity is defined as the value of the last unit one is willing to spend money or time and attention on. Although this principle can by no means be applied to everything we do (a lot of activities, such as saxophone playing, become more rewarding the more one carries on), it can offer important insights into the situation Bourdieu describes – how news, and more generally information, is being produced and consumed. In this regard, it is easy to see that stronger effects are needed eventually, because the public becomes accustomed to speed and explosive forms of communication.

At the same time – and this is more important here – the people who actually produce news and other kinds of information, the journalists that is, experience the increasing crowdedness of their field.

Readers, listeners and viewers have less and less time to spare for each information snippet. Thus, editors working in every kind of press (from web and WAP to paper) cut more and more. As an occasional contributor to the press and sometimes an interviewee, I have never heard an editor complain that a particular piece of journalism is too short, to say the least. (One may, naturally, dream: 'Look, this interview that you have done, isn't it a bit on the short side? I mean, didn't he say other things as well? He comes through as a man of bombast and one-liners, wouldn't it be better to allow the nuances in his position to come through, in order to avoid his being misunderstood, and then we'll also avoid a stupid and irrelevant controversy in the paper afterwards. Will you give me another hundred lines before lunch tomorrow?')

News on WAP, at the time of writing the latest vogue in accelerated journalism, offers stories of a length that makes those in the *Mirror* look like Proust. As a compensation, they can be updated every 30 minutes. To those of us who are not yet accustomed to this speed and brevity, this kind of journalism is like a persistent insect buzzing around the ear as we try to go to sleep. (WAP news = the mosquito problem in equatorial Africa.) Yet there is a marked tendency for such strategies to win, for reasons already elaborated. The marginal value of information falls dramatically after a certain number of images or words; it is pretty high during the first 10 seconds, but then what?

The most common objection to this line of reasoning is that slowness seems to be enjoying a renaissance in the media, at least in some European countries. For example, dedicated radio channels play classical music 24 hours a day, and there is a 'perceived need' (the pundits claim) for thorough, decent reasoning and solid journalism providing background information. This may well be the case in the world as it appears from Islington, but hardly from Fleet Street. Sales of broadsheets decline, while those of tabloids (which look more and more like printed television) increase. The people enjoying the 'slowness renaissance' can be counted in tenths of per cents, and on this scale there may be slight increases here and there; fastness is enjoyed by groups better measured in scores of per cents. In Norway, a radio programme that allowed academics to read out 30-minute talks, called the *P2 Academy*, has been on the air for more than five years, and it covers black holes, juvenile delinquency, the concept of culture and similar issues authoritatively and well. The listeners love it. Both of them.

INFORMATION LINT DESTROYS CONTINUITY

Fast thinkers are favoured, and the slow thinkers sulk, in some cases reacting through producing essays like Bourdieu's. He is far from alone; his attack on contemporary journalism stands in a proud lineage of socialist and conservative intellectuals decrying the vulgarity of mass-produced information. This tradition may have begun with de Tocqueville's assault on the pragmatic, democratic and superficial North American settler culture (although, if one reads him closely, Plato had something to say on the matter as well), but reached its zenith with the Frankfurt School of the inter-war years – Marcuse, Horkheimer and, especially, Adorno. German Jews in the 1930s certainly had their own reasons for pessimism. This does not mean that they were necessarily wrong. When Neil Postman writes that today's students no longer use the word 'because' in their exam papers, he points towards the same problem as Bourdieu discusses, which is further illustrated by the list at p. 109. Coherence and causality slip away when it is restlessness, flickering gazes and striking one-liners that rule the roost. In his recent memoir, Johan Galtung – otherwise a relentless optimist – writes this about his experiences with students in the 1990s:

> And far too many suffer from chronic image flicker, a synchronic experience of reality as images rich in details, not as lines across time, causal chains, reasoning. One needs both, but the way it is today, the ability to think is slowly killed, to the advantage of the ability to see and hear, taste and feel – an orgy of the senses that gives little space for intellectuality.

In a recent report about the state of higher education in Norway, the committee has included a passage about 'those students who choose to study full-time'. As if studying was not primarily a full-time activity! As a matter of fact, most teachers at the university or polytechnic level in Europe have experienced a gradual change here since the 1970s. The cost of living and consumption expectations have gone up, and most students are obliged to take wage-work. Formerly, students primarily worked during the vacations, eventually weekend and evening work became more common, and presently it is my impression that work and studies are best seen as a seamless whole where it is difficult to tell which activity is deemed the most important. In recent years, I have had increasing problems arranging supervision meetings with postgraduate students because they have problems getting away from work. Studying is no longer simply what it is that one does, but an entry on the total menu of experiences that composes the life of a young, urban and unattached person. This result is not, naturally, the students' fault. Like all of us, they are victims of vertical stacking. The range of activities that compete with studying grows every semester. There is always something urgent that needs to be done first, before one sits down with *The Phenomenology of Spirit* for six months or so. As every good academic knows, thorough learning of a complex curriculum requires long, continuous periods of concentration, insomnia and anxiety, reduced appetite for sustained periods, problems in one's love life, absentmindedness and aloofness from contemporary matters. (And in the old days, we would have added: lots of strong filter coffee and tobacco.) This kind of student is still around, but the great majority is of a different kind. When they appear in the lecture room, they are on their way from one place to another; they have a wide spectrum of activities to fill their days with, from clubbing to wage-work, television zapping, web surfing and being with friends. If they want to be abreast with their surroundings and strengthen their career opportunities, they simply cannot disengage themselves for years of a slow, monk-like existence. In the labour market, attractive applicants have CVs which indicate diverse experience and high speed.

This new situation in academia – the falling marginal value of slowly acquired knowledge – also entails that it can no longer be taken for granted that the most brilliant students will be interested in pursuing a career in research and teaching. Universities may either adapt themselves to the market (which is largely what is happening, certainly in the UK and Scandinavia) and speed up their teaching, or they may redefine themselves as countercultural institutions that embody slowness, thoroughness and afterthoughts.

The students' situation is comparable to my own, although my research time is not chopped up into useless fragments because of a pressing need for external wage-work, cinema and concert attendance, evenings on the town and so on – but because of the prevalence of *information lint*. This includes tasks like replying to e-mail, answering the phone, filing, responding to letters, booking flights, reading half-baked reports and other kinds of bureaucratic documents, and so on. Before one is finally able to sit down with something that might make a difference, there is always something else that needs to be done first. What is given priority in a situation where one has many tasks waiting to be done, is either the first task that comes to mind or that which simply cannot wait. Not unsurprisingly, quite a few academics plan major works that never get beyond the drawing-board. Academic books increasingly look like cut-and-paste collages with snippets of conference papers here and excerpts of journal articles there. We always have 5 minutes to spare for a given task, often even half an hour, but never five years. Since the growth in information is much, much faster than population growth, there is inevitably more to relate to for each of us (in particular, those of us who are positioned as information switchboards). The marginal value of new information is nearly zero, and it is therefore easier to attract a crumb of attention if one wraps the information in packages of ever decreasing size. Little packages that are stacked on top of each other to create wavering, thin towers that are soon tall enough to touch the moon.

The nimble stacking of blocks of decreasing size is a craft which spreads in many directions. Rhythmic dance music, the World Wide Web, multi-channel television, journalism, studies and research are some of the examples that have been mentioned here. One can increasingly combine the blocks according to whim (this is why techno music is such a telling example). This process can only to some extent be quantified and 'proved'; its results can only be experienced. More and more of every kind of information is stacked, like gigantic Lego towers where the bricks have nothing in common but the fact that they fit (but they also fit with any other brick). It is not because of the phenomenal global success of Nestlé's main coffee product that the term *instant* is a key concept for an attempt to understand the present age. The moment, or instant, is ephemeral, superficial and intense. When the moment (or even the *next* moment) dominates our being in time, we no longer have space for building blocks that can only be used for one or a few configurations with other blocks. Everything must be interchangeable with everything else *now*. The entry ticket has to be cheap, the initial investment modest. Swift changes and unlimited flexibility are main assets. In the last instance, everything that is left is a single, overfilled, compressed, eternal moment. Supposing this point is reached some time in the future, and both past and future are fully erased, we would definitely have reached an absolute limit (recall Virilio: 'There are no delays any more'). It is difficult to imagine this happening – there are many universal human experiences that only make sense as duration. However, in several fields, the tendency towards extreme compression of time is evident; some of them perhaps unexpected, such as consumption, work and the very formation of personal identity. That is the topic of the next chapter, which shows some effects of the tyranny of the moment on aspects of life which have no direct relationship to the Internet, trance music or accelerated journalism.

7   The Lego Brick Syndrome

Work expands to fill the time available for its completion
(Parkinson's Law, 1955)

A typical working day in my life begins as I unlock the office, turn on the coffee machine and my Macintosh, playing stored messages from the answering machine as I jot down numbers to be dialled during the day, often before taking off my coat. I then open my electronic mailbox and go through the morning's first batch of e-mail, before collecting the other kind of mail from my pigeon-hole. The stack of mail might contain some direct marketing blurb from publishers, a couple of requests for talks, and a couple of dozen tables of contents from professional journals one ought to read regularly to keep updated. Then on to the Usenet, where I participate in eight or nine so-called discussion groups where global discussions relevant for my work are carried on. In between, I try to read a couple of newspapers.

During the day I might send, say, between three and six faxes and receive as many, send and receive about five e-mails, have ten to fifteen telephone conversations and write three to four letters. As a matter of fact, most of the day is spent on this kind of task. And still I haven't even begun to contemplate doing that which ultimately gives my presence in the office a purpose, namely research, teaching and popularisation in the discipline which is my profession. I rarely find the time to think two thoughts in succession, let alone read two consecutive pages, during office hours. In order to write a longer text than a newspaper article, many academics are forced to use weekends, vacations and late evenings – preferably without a telephone line nearby.

These were the opening paragraphs of a newspaper article I wrote way back in 1995. There have been a few changes since then. I no longer take part in Usenet newsgroups, nor do I subscribe to listservs; as a perverted kind of compensation, I receive much, much more e-mail today. But I hardly send faxes any more, and the amount of cellulose mail has also decreased. Such details apart, I cannot deny that the above description would on the whole be quite appropriate even today – and not just for me, but for thousands upon thousands

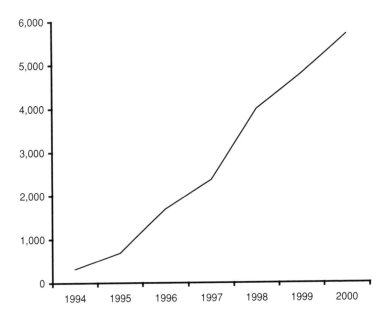

Figure 7.1 E-mail received annually by T.H.E., 1994–2000

of people who are in varying ways affected by the side-effects of information society. This chapter is devoted to them (us), regarded not just as producers and consumers, but also occasionally as persons. But first, a small detour.

Zeno of Elea, who lived in the sixth century BC, was one of the most gifted pupils to sit in the olive grove with the philosopher Parmenides. The Master had taught him that movement is really an illusion – contrary to common sense, everything actually stood perfectly still – and Zeno tried to prove that Parmenides was right. He did so through his four paradoxes, the most famous of which is the story about Achilles and the tortoise.

A race had been organised between Achilles and the tortoise. The tortoise was naturally sluggish in its movements, while athletic Achilles was in Olympic form. However, the tortoise was given an initial advantage of a few metres. Therefore, says Zeno, it became theoretically impossible for Achilles to overtake it. First he would have to run to the point where the tortoise was when he started, but by then it would have moved on. Then he would have to run to this point, but again, the tortoise would have crawled on a bit. And so on *ad infinitum*. Each time Achilles reached the point where the tortoise was a little while earlier, it would have moved a little bit further. The distance was obviously greatly reduced as the race went on – it approached zero – but Achilles could in principle never overtake the tortoise.

Although Aristotle, who lived two centuries later, was convinced that Zeno was wrong (and it is easy to regard this point of view with a certain sympathy), the paradox was not resolved satisfactorily until Henri Bergson, in his first treatise, *Time and Free Will,* introduced a sharp distinction between time and space. According to Bergson time, regarded as duration, had nothing to do with space, and Zeno's baffling paradoxes (another famous one is to do with an arrow 'which appears to move') were a result of his misleading creation of 'points in time', that is spatialisations of time, which in Bergson's view were misleading.

Many of my earlier examples of acceleration and stacking can be read as oblique (not to say perverse) footnotes to Zeno's most famous paradox. He called attention to the relationship between time and space. His conclusion was that movement was theoretically impossible and therefore had to be an illusion. (Anyone wondering why philosophers have a reputation for being out of touch with real life?) This conclusion is not pertinent here, but, at the same time, it is clear that the relationship between time and space has undergone dramatic changes caused largely by innovations in communication technology. Theoreticians have proposed fancy concepts to deal with this: Jean Baudrillard talks of the *implosion of the time/space axis,* Anthony Giddens says that there has been a *collapse of the time/space coordinates,* Manuel Castells writes about how *the space of flows has replaced the space of places,* David Harvey speaks of *time–space compression,* and so on.

It is no longer viable to pretend that a certain duration corresponds to a certain distance. For this reason, delays, gaps and slowness as such are threatened in ways I have indicated in preceding chapters. Allow me on this background to update and rephrase Zeno's paradox as Eriksen's paradox: *When time is chopped up into sufficiently small units, it ceases to exist* . That is to say, it ceases to exist as duration (which presupposes that events take a certain time), but continues to exist as *moments about to be overtaken by the next moment.* The same pattern can be observed in many, apparently unrelated fields. Until quite recently, we were faced with choices between a limited number of 'personal identity packages', which were fairly well defined: either I am one of these, or I am one of those. Either I go into shipping like my uncle, or I find a more meaningful job with the Salvation Army. Either I am a real lefty with long hair, round spectacles and a critical view of NATO and nuclear power, or I am a slick Tory type with navy blue blazers and conformist opinions about everything from child-raising to taxation and military issues.

In this kind of situation (which could, perhaps, be labelled 'modern'), each and every one of us, citizens of liberal, individualist countries, received a box of colourful Lego bricks at birth, furnished with a number of specific instructions for their assembly: choose one! Nowadays (in a situation which could, perhaps, be labelled 'postmodern'), it is more as if we receive the same box of Lego bricks, but the sets of instructions – alas – are long lost, and moreover, we seem to be forced to re-build or at least modify our wavering constructions every day. This must be what Giddens had in mind when, in *Modernity and Self-Identity*, he spoke of *the self as a project*: it is not a given entity, it has to be created again and again. Tendencies to this effect can be observed in otherwise very different areas, such as personal identity (who am I *really?*), work and professional careers, family life, consumer habits, taste and political convictions. I shall now proceed to show how the fixation on the moment, stacking and the Lego brick syndrome influence the central spheres of life in our societies; labour, family life, leisure, consumption. It will be indicated how changes that have bearings on these pillars of contemporary life are expressions of a pattern that has already been described from different points of view, under the headings acceleration, stacking and exponential growth.

AN ACCELERATED PROFESSIONAL LIFE OFFERS FLEXIBILITY AND REMOVES SECURITY

In an important and influential little book about the new economy and its effects on ways of life and personal identity, *The Corrosion of Character*, Richard Sennett describes how successful people in the emergent economy of the 1990s – flexible, adjustable, technologically capable people – experienced a vacuum in the very centre of their lives. He does not talk of the generic 'nerd' type who never gets married and who, according to the myth, has underdeveloped social skills, but about decent, ordinary professionals who 'struggle to have a life', as they say in the USA. They work within sectors such as finance, web design, e-commerce, advertising, journalism and so on, and there are many of them. To some extent, they work in companies of a kind that did not exist ten or twenty years ago, to some extent in sectors that have been radically transformed because of the computer revolution. There is a major difference between the job of a foreign correspondent today, in the age of digital video and satellite television, and the 'same job' say, at the time when Evelyn Waugh wrote *Scoop* (1938). Consider also the difference between working in telecommunications before 1990 and today: in the old days, telecommunications were chiefly about telephone poles and cables. The engineers of the state-controlled telecom companies boasted, in the case of difficult countries like Norway (mountainous, with a jagged coastline and scattered population), that they had achieved a telephone coverage of 99 per cent thanks to costly, but enduring investments in a valuable infrastructure. Ten years later, telecom people talk about web portals, and their field is now based on satellite communication; SMS messages, mobile telephony, Internet and video conferencing. Since the mid-1990s, the number of mobile telephone subscriptions sold globally has exceeded the number of stationary subscriptions. For countries like China, it will never be an option to build a material network of poles and cables criss-crossing the entire country to ensure a coverage of, say, 99 per cent.

The example of telecommunications is apt because it works two ways: on the one hand, this kind of technology makes up the backbone of the new society, and plays a decisive role in the new labour market, the emerging patterns of consumption and communication, and so on. At the same time, it is also itself a part of the labour market that has suddenly been forced to adapt to new circumstances, with obvious consequences for employees. Old-timers with long and varied experience do not have a high market value in this new setting.

Sennett describes people who have been liberated from the monotonous drudgery of the conveyor belt and the time recorder. They have flexible jobs. They travel extensively, they send and receive lots of e-mail, and as a part of their labour contract, their mobile phone is always turned on. They have in most cases moved several times to advance their career (North Americans in general tend to be less sedentary than Europeans). They live under constant pressure to reinvent themselves, update and change their perspectives on the job they are doing, turn around quickly and change their strategies. There is little that smacks of routine in their work. Researching the book, Sennett spoke to a handful of people, and most of them did not yearn for the relatively stable, predictable situation that characterised work a generation ago. They enjoy the flexibility and opportunities of the new economy (opportunities that are largely confined to a minority, but one which is growing quickly). Yet they experience serious problems in attempting to make their lives hang together as something other than a discontinuous series of events, career moves and so on.

Some of them are virtually burnt out before they are 35. (Burnt out is, incidentally, an excellent metaphor: heat is, physically speaking, nothing but speed.) In Norway, the growth in sick leave from 1999 to 2000 was an unhealthy 12 per cent. According to the Prime Minister, in a bid to justify cuts in the 2001 state budget, the country would have saved the equivalent of nearly £1,000,000,000 if government spending on sick leave and temporary disability benefits were only brought down to the 1998 level! (We are, remember, talking about a country with 4.5 million inhabitants in all!) According to the *Guardian*, 40 per cent of American workers report that they perceive their job as 'very or extremely stressful'. Stress is not the same as having a lot to do, but being unable to do one's work before one has to do other things first. In the UK, 30 per cent of the workforce report that they experience mental health problems, and in Germany, 7 per cent take early retirement because they are stressed and depressed. Early burn-out is already in a good position to contend for the title of the civilisational disease of the new century.

The new technology, and the shift of the gravitational point in the economy from industry to information, imply that many workers actually are in a position to evade the nine-to-five routine. They can work at home, in a plane (or, more likely, in an airport waiting for a delayed plane), in the park or in the car. Physical presence during working hours is no longer seen as a necessity. They may not need to be on time any more, but instead they are expected to be online.

Sennett does not mention it, but he might well have: the use of anti-depressant and related substances grew spectacularly in the USA of the 1990s, closely following the development of 'the new economy'. The number of prescriptions for so-called psycho-active medicines in the US went from 131 million in 1988 to 233 million in 1998. One single product, Prozac, was prescribed to 10 million sufferers in 1998. In addition, millions of North Americans take herbal medicines and other prescription-free stimulants (including cocaine and amphetamines) to improve their sense of well-being. The psychiatrist Randolph Nesse has speculated on the possibility that the strong optimism characterising the US economy, and particularly the exceptionally widespread financial risk-taking associated with rather airy Internet projects, might be directly connected to the fact that these substances neutralise fear and anxiety. Is the continuous boom lasting from 1992 to the present a result of Prozac? Hard, but Nesse's view is also far from irrelevant.

THE DISTINCTION BETWEEN WORK AND LEISURE IS ERASED

Work wins. When the notions of working from home and 'distance working' were introduced in the early 1990s, employers worried that they might lose control over their workers' activities. Perhaps they suspected that instead of working, their employees would lie on the couch sipping beer and watching soap operas, given new opportunities entailed by weakened direct surveillance. The second half of the 1990s indicated that other anxieties are more to the point. The new flexibility quietly, but inevitably erases the boundary between work and leisure. Since one of the most general principles of speed states that fast time always wins over slow time when they meet on an equal footing, it requires only a modest feat of the imagination to see that labour wins over leisure, and not the other way around, when they meet in a particular site. In this way, people can actually be 'at work' always if they so wish, or if the kind of work they do requires it.

The expectation that one should be available as a potentially working person at any time, is an important dimension of new work. Complete availability is contagious. When some firms or individuals begin, others have to follow suit lest they lose their competitive edge. The other day I heard about a man in his thirties, who was being watched by my informant as he kicked a ball in the park with his son, who was around 6. During the half hour the ball game lasted, he did not once remove the cellphone from his right ear.

New career structures are also an important part of the new economy. The era of gold watches is gone, and it will probably not return. In the old days (until say, 1985), many would begin to work for a company after completing their education (which could be very early in life back then). Then one made one's slow career moves following the rules of seniority, merit and proximity to the powers that be. After 25 years of loyal service to the company, one was reasonably well placed in its pyramidal hierarchy, and the managing director would rise from his enormous mahogany desk and descend to offer a gold watch with the company's insignia engraved on it.

Today, it is instead the case that one is more or less a *loser* (that terrible American word) out of touch with the contemporary economy if one stays in the same job for more than a couple of years. Exaggerations aside, it is well documented that it is becoming increasingly rare that employees work full-time in the same company for the greater part of their professional life. Part-time and flexitime work, freelancing, outsourcing, independent consultancies and frequent changes of work have become part and parcel of the economy's structure, not just in the USA, but in places like Scandinavia and Britain as well.

Seen from the perspective of the company, it has become a crucial challenge for the leadership to find ways of persuading good workers to stay. In the changing new economy, there are many alternatives for people with saleable skills. Restlessness is the Siamese twin of flexibility. They enjoy each other's company.

Finally, the distinction between short-term and long-term planning seems to have been eradicated in many companies. All planning has to be short-term, for nobody knows what the world will look like (the markets, the target groups, the clients, the students...) in five or even three years.

This is not tantamount to saying that things used to be better. By no means. I would not have preferred to live in the inter-war years or the 1950s. The new flexibility of work does create genuine choice and freedom. The hierarchical, static organisational models typical of the classic industrial era are increasingly being replaced – with enormous difficulties, it must be conceded – by network-based, project-oriented models where the structure of the organisation is determined by the tasks at hand, not by the organisational map. There are a variety of forms of attachment to a company, and this can in many cases depend just as much on the employee's wishes as on the company's own strategies. The values of individualism and choice are taken to new heights, and this is not in itself a bad thing.

Yet the new economy has a number of unintended consequences for those directly affected by it, some of them distinctly unpleasant. First of all, the new work makes firms and workers alike extremely vulnerable. The rate of change, turbulence, speed and freedom from the life-long labour contract with its clocking-in machines and gold watches provide freedom, but also serve as a reminder that the underside of freedom nearly always is loss of security.

Second, today's work tends to favour (and boost) a particular set of personality traits. Adaptability, openness, a speedy style of working and opportunism pay off both economically and in other ways. If anyone wonders why the teaching profession has been relegated to a backwater (poor recruitment, low salaries and declining social position), this is the answer. The work of a teacher is by necessity a slow and cumulative activity based on a relatively stable set of values. Its ideals are far removed from those of the new era.

For those who are wholly or partly immersed in the new economy, the sense that the world is no longer coherently interconnected may be the most important side-effect. Neither optimism nor pessimism is prevalent in visions of the near future these days; it seems fundamentally open and uncertain. A main cause is that the present is oblique and difficult to conceptualise. It could also be said that no particular direction emerges from this present time, narcissistically obsessed with itself and terrorised by the demands of the next moment.

Sennett is particularly interested in the relationship between different spheres of life, notably work and family. His informants say things like, 'I am extremely busy and overworked right now, and I do not have enough time for my family, but this is going to improve very soon.' This, any expert on management can confirm, executives are apt to say at brief intervals throughout their careers. These days, however, such difficulties are not the exclusive domain of busy and well-paid executives. Employees in many areas and at many levels – journalists, academics, salespeople, bureaucrats, publishers... all feel that the fast time of work is cannibalising the slow time of private life. And as work is being parcelled up into ever decreasing segments along several dimensions (the turnover of jobs, tasks, routines, etc. becomes faster and faster), and demands growing chunks of the individual employee, the logic of private life becomes dated and problematic. Family life, in particular, seems to demand a kind of time which is difficult to reconcile with professional careers. It is easy enough to see the symptoms of this, both in relationships between spouses and in the child–parent relationship.

This is not a covert way of moralising over the growing divorce rates in Western Europe. Indeed, high divorce rates may be an indication of an improved quality of life. When it is easy to get a divorce and there are few cultural sanctions against it, which is now the case in Northern Europe, it becomes a realistic option to get out of unbearable marriages. Women especially seem to have benefited from changes in this field (most divorces are initiated by women), men and children to a lesser degree.

Gregory Bateson was deeply interested in the concept of flexibility. In an essay from the early 1970s, he argues that the more energy that is harnessed for human activities, the less flexible a society is. He thereby turns a notion from human ecology on its head, namely the idea (which stems from Leslie White) that the 'evolutionary level' of a society can be seen as a function of its efficiency in exploiting available energy resources. In Bateson's view, the result of efficient exploitation is not so much that society advances, but that possible options are closed off. After the agricultural revolution and its accompanying population growth, there was no possibility of return to hunting and gathering. After the Industrial Revolution and its dependency on clock time, the synchronisation of millions of people and high energy consumption, it is difficult to envision a return to the less temporally disciplined and interdependent agricultural society, and so on.

The Batesonian notion of flexibility can easily be adapted to shed light on the topic at hand. Flexibility in time use implies that there is vacant time, empty time, time available which has not been efficiently filled with specified activities or a specified kind of information input. Time for meandering thoughts, for slow activities with no instrumental aim and no fixed duration, time for just fooling around. Before the life of the European student became crowded with wage-work, leisure and short courses, student life entailed a real possibility of wandering leisurely about in the halls of learning, and discovering the unexpected. When course reading increasingly becomes geared towards the upcoming exams (which are rarely far away), and time for reading as such becomes more scarce, it is increasingly difficult for a student to make independent discoveries. Extra-curricular reading becomes an unnecessary and therefore unprioritised luxury. Creativity disappears.

Bateson notes that increased flexibility in one area tends to remove flexibility elsewhere. If this could be seen as a general principle, it might explain why it is that the flexibility of 'new work' touted by business pundits and some social scientists as a massive improvement on the routine nine-to-five drudgery, takes flexibility away from everything else. Family life is Taylorised, leisure becomes infused with work, the gaps are filled with little tasks. Or, on a more general note, it could be stated that the enormous flexibility currently witnessed in the dissemination of information takes flexibility out of people's time, which becomes more overfilled than ever before.

FAMILY LIFE IS BY NATURE SLOW AND FITS THE CURRENT ERA BADLY

More or less frequent changes of life partners are clear indications of the spread of the tyranny of the moment into the intimate sphere, no matter how one prefers to judge the tendency morally. The classic Christian notion 'until death do us part' did contain an important safety valve: one was liberated and free to remarry if the spouse died. In earlier times, this alternative was a realistic one for a lot of people. Yet marriage was considered to be enduring and not least *slow*. Indians, who generally live in arranged marriages and hesitate to get divorced, may put it like this: 'Western marriages begin when love is at the boiling point, and then the temperature goes down gradually, year by year. Our marriages begin when we scarcely know each other, with rather lukewarm emotions on both sides, but then they slowly heat up like a water kettle on low heat.' Like a novel, a treatise or a linear television series, the logic of marriage dictates that it should be more like the Indian model than the Western one: it goes through a series of phases, each of which builds on the preceding phase. Couples share 'good and bad days' together; both partners eventually grow older, they develop annoying quirks, they become bald, fat or wrinkled, and it must indeed frequently seem that the grass is greener on the other side. However, when the threshold for a change of partner is lowered, one of several results is that a great number of people never get to experience particular phases (or stages) in their intimate relationships. They go back to square one again and again, with new bursts of sleepless nights, beating hearts and uncertainty; eventually with new children, new parents-in-law, new mortgages, new tortuous trips to IKEA (at least in my part of the world), new heated arguments about which Christmas customs are to be considered legitimate and so on. Seen in this light, serial monogamy is one of the best extant examples of life's tendency to stand still at great speed around the turn of the millennium. We happily return to square one, priding ourselves on our ability to 'remain young', and maturity becomes an outlandish concept.

Marriages are under direct pressure from the tyranny of the moment, which demands unmediated, instant gratification, which promises ever new and more exciting moments, and which militates against the values associated with history, connectedness and duration. The pressure comes from both within and outside. Dissolved marriages are one easily quantifiable aspect of the pressure on the family; another possible implication of new work and its associated acceleration is the relegation of family life to a residual category, a kind of spare tank of time to be filled or emptied depending on the number of other activities to hand. As the family has been 'emptied of functions' (a lament heard from sociologists for 30 years), it becomes increasingly difficult, within the new economy, to understand what it is for. Put slightly differently, the number of Bridget Joneses and characters such as those depicted by Nick Hornby – immature and unfixed Peter Pans of both genders, often well into their thirties – is clearly on the rise.

The family is riddled with uncertainties regarding its functions. A major preoccupation for many parents is the industrial organisation of family time. It goes like this: if you take X to her violin lesson today, I will go and collect Y at kindergarten. If you take both of them to the country at the weekend so that I can get down to doing something, I'll take them to my parents next weekend. Can you stay at home today, so that I can go to that meeting? If I can leave early for work tomorrow, you can do it on Thursday. Deal!

In this way, family life is being Taylorised; it acquires the characteristics of assembly line production – while working life simultaneously becomes more varied, more demanding and richer in its promises of personal fulfilment.

Family deliberations about the organisation of time can be carried out in impeccably democratic ways – which is, at least, an advance over undiluted competition: one moves, as it were, from the ruthless struggles of economics to the compromises of politics; and this method must also be seen as an advance on old-fashioned patriarchy. On the deficit side, it is not easy to invest a profound sense of meaning into family life when balancing the daily time budgets has become a major ingredient. There exists, I am inclined to believe, no other social arena where long duration and slow time are more important, and therefore under stronger pressure, than the family sphere. Many employers in the new economy know this.

They therefore prefer to employ single people, who can be persuaded to work more or less all day when necessary. Perhaps they even give their new employees a mobile phone with a fully paid subscription, so that they can phone them on Sunday morning, ordering them to report to the office immediately.

The external framing of contemporary family life in this setting is the logic of the moment, and it is directly opposed to the logic of the family. Family life is neither particularly labour-intensive nor capital-intensive, but it is extremely time-intensive. The parody is that phenomenon which is called 'quality time' with the children, where the busy father or mother enjoys 15 minutes of qualitatively outstanding time with the kids every evening at bedtime. In an age when both men and women participate fully in a tight and demanding labour market, and the distinction between work and leisure is becoming blurred, at the same time as gender roles are uncertain and contested (nobody can tell unequivocally what it means to be a good man or a good woman any more), it is far from easy to find an existential rhythm where the particular qualities of family life – slowness, organic growth, trust – are allowed to flourish.

These considerations are not particularly original. The family as a form of life is nevertheless faced with other, less theorised, problems caused by the tyranny of the moment.

The first problem is to do with the transmission of knowledge. It does not just affect parents, but teachers of every kind up to university level. When culture changes quickly, in some people's view so fast that it loses its footing, then it is not easy to see what the young ought to learn from their parental generation. The wisdom of the parents, based on years of experience, is not necessarily perceived as relevant. What could a person born in the 1940s teach someone born in the 1970s about personal computers and their use? How can an older person in their forties even contemplate explaining the challenges of multi-ethnicity to a 15-year-old? And what do mum and dad really know about the importance of travelling to the Far East and Latin America before one goes on to university, or why any healthy teenage girl has to send several SMS messages every day to her friends in order to remain in touch and not be socially isolated; or, for that matter, how idiotic the belief in politics as a means to societal change is? The faster and more encompassing changes are, the more problematic the transmission of culture between the generations becomes. Or, differently put: in this situation, children and adolescents are increasingly free to fashion their own values and their own meaningful lives, pulling together fragments from various sources, ranging from the varied input of schoolteachers to the latest Nintendo game. Duration and continuity lose out; spontaneity and innovation win. The Lego blocks are, as mentioned, liberated from any set of instructions. Whether this is good or bad, naturally depends on the content. Only people who either lack values or who have neglected to reflect on the matter, would seriously hold that innovation is *per se* good. The gas chambers were an innovation.

THE CULT OF YOUTH IS CAUSED BY THE TYRANNY OF THE MOMENT

The second problem, connected to the first, is the extremely widespread cultivation of youthfulness. In nearly all non-modern societies, adulthood, maturity and even old age are associated with high rank. It is as a grown man or woman with one's own children, an established career in productive work and a secure sense of self that one achieves trusted positions in society and commands the deference of others. A main, understudied difference between Europeans and non-European immigrants is the tendency of the latter to retire at an earlier age, often barely into their fifties. This should not be taken to indicate laziness. In that phase of modernity that developed in the decades after the Second World War, it has become an established virtue to 'stay young' as long as possible. Before the Second World War, it was still common in northern Scandinavia for 15-year-olds to receive, as confirmation gifts, a silver cigarette case and a set of false teeth (often made of whale ivory), as symbols of adulthood. They were now old enough to go to sea or find other independent employment, and were generally considered independent persons, at least in the working class. People were barely out of their teens before they married and had children. They could hardly wait to grow up and be in charge of their own lives.

Since then, the boundaries between life stages have become increasingly fuzzy. The category of 'youth', that intermediate stage between childhood and adulthood, has expanded in both directions. Children who have barely begun school form a core market for strongly sexualised pop music and a style of dress that until recently was the exclusive domain of teenagers, while men and women in their forties are being told from almost every direction that it would be great if they could stay young and cool just a little longer, perhaps helping nature a little bit with a facelift, a hair transplant or some liposuction, and generally make certain not to stop adapting to their surroundings. As a consequence, they continue feeling uncertain and unstable in their personal identity a little longer, and become the grateful victims of all kinds of marketing of lifestyle products. As someone remarked in a conversation recently, Christopher Lasch's devastating critique of contemporary culture, *The Culture of Narcissism*, was fine when it was published, but it is only now that it is truly needed.

Two of the most serious symptoms of the tyranny of the moment are these: the cult of youth and the crisis in knowledge transmission. A culture that does not value maturity and ageing also does not care where it comes from, and can therefore be quite clueless as to where it is heading.

In every society, adult life is associated with responsibility, pre-dictability and stable commitments. An adult knows who he or she is, which values are the most important, and – in most cases – has clear responsibilities for children and spouse, often in-laws and own parents in addition. When one is young, on the contrary, one is unfixed, uncertain, playful and has an experimental view of life, implying a fundamental openness to the opportunities that might present themselves. One has not yet committed oneself to a particular direction. Translated into the clichés of our time, this means that the young (or youthful) person is flexible and ready for new challenges. Who would not rather employ this kind of individual than a predictable person who is certain of his priorities?

In the new economy it may be correct – at least in the short run – that the values we associate with youthfulness are a recipe for success. But in other spheres – family, the arts, personal development – it is a disaster. In nearly all cultures, adolescence is perceived as a societal challenge. Precisely because the persons in question are 'betwixt and between', they are personally uncertain of their identity, their duties and entitlements; and at the same time they represent a threat to the continuity of society's values. The contem-porary taste for young executives indicates that love of the fleeting moment is currently greater than respect for the long lines of history. The transitional, turbulent mode of youth has become the mainstay of society.

The youth cult makes a mess of categories since every age is reduced to the same ideals. When both the 8-year-old daughter and the 42-year-old father regard themselves as 'young people', it is not easy to establish an unambiguous parental relationship. When I grew up in the late 1960s and early 1970s, mothers still carried handbags and wore conservative coats. A short decade earlier, fathers still wore trenchcoats, hats and ties. They would not be caught dead in jeans on a weekday. The main cause of the youth cult is the acceleration in cultural change, which implies that it makes more sense to have a lot of spontaneous energy than a lot of accumulated history in one's portfolio, it fits the new economy perfectly, it affects family life adversely, and the blame is usually put on advertising and the entertainment industry. Admittedly, it is striking how young and beautiful people with Colgate smiles, silicone in the right places and a self-confident body language dominate central cultural arenas such as pop music, advertisements, North American films and televised weather forecasts. (Not entirely though: I can easily envision the conversation between the weary father and the pre-pubescent daughter, ending with the daughter's ultimatum: 'All right dad, I will go to that Phil Collins concert with you, but on one condition: I want silicone in my lips first.') As a general description, however, this diagnosis is inevitable. If anything, the icons of popular culture have become younger (and thinner, therefore faster) during the most recent decades. But to blame such surface phenomena is tantamount to confounding the menu with the food. Popular culture can be good or bad, conventional or innovative; but it is always a reflex of underlying patterns. In earlier chapters I have shown how technological change has side-effects that, among other things, stimulate the cult of youth. Incidentally, Paul Virilio, whose analysis in *The Information Bomb* closely parallels this line of argument, differs slightly in that he sees contemporary culture not primarily as pubescent, but as infantile. To him, the 'man-child' Bill Gates with his unworried fascination for advanced toys, is the quintessential embodiment of a global culture which uncritically takes on the childish aspects of American culture.

An essential arena in this context is that of consumption. A classic definition of a society's economy divides it into three institutions: production, distribution and consumption. The recent move from production to consumption as the focal point of Western economies is aptly illustrated in the refurbishing – actually total redefinition – of areas such as the Docklands in London (and many cities have their equivalents) from industry to shops and flats. It is evident that the role of the consumer has grown in importance during the latter half of the twentieth century, and that the war over the free seconds and pence in the lives of consumers is being intensified every fleeting moment.

CONSUMPTION IS STACKED, AND COHERENCE DISAPPEARS

It is easy to prove that the material standard of living improved in all industrial countries during the last half-century; whether there has been a similar growth in the quality of life, is more open to discussion. Still, we use commodities of roughly the same kind as the parental generation (with some exceptions, such as spam, boiled cabbage and flannel trousers), and in addition, we consume more, and more, and even more. The tendency continues. People in their twenties are deeply conversant with a telephone technology that slightly older men and women will never become acquainted with (the SMS message). Shopping has become an everyday activity for the middle classes everywhere in the rich countries – virtually a form of recreation. (And it seems far from unlikely that many people, most of them women, acquire some sorely needed hours of slow time by strolling aimlessly around in large shopping centres.)

Economic growth, which the world has seen to an almost unprecedented degree since the early 1990s, presupposes a growth in consumption. It can either be achieved through finding new markets or by making the already existing consumers intensify their consumption. Both options are being exploited. For a while it was predicted that the new shopping centres that mushroomed near highway junctions in various European countries would lead to mass bankruptcy among high street shops. So far, this has generally not come about. There seems to be room for everyone, in addition to the new e-shops, which are still only just beginning.

For people to be able to consume more, they must either replace their existing items more frequently or diversify their selection of commodities. In this field, as in other areas, it is correct to state that both things are happening. Both clothes and capital goods have decreasing lifespans, and besides, a home in 2001 contains many more objects than a similar home would have in 1981. The selection grows everywhere, not just within the field of information. A while ago, a green variety of ketchup was introduced. The producer was also contemplating a blue variety, but the children in the test panel disliked it. This kind of diversification can be observed nearly everywhere: breakfast cereals, garden furniture, shirts, light bulbs, taco sauces, potato crisps, milk, detergents, holiday destinations... the exceptions, such as when the selection range is reduced because mighty companies like Microsoft and Coca-Cola successfully achieve near-monopolies with their products, are fewer than Marx might have guessed.

The Swedish economist Staffan Linder made a study of this phenomenon in the late 1960s, entitled *The Harried Leisure Class*. Linder, a conservative critic of consumer culture, held that the inbuilt demands for growth in capitalism made it necessary for each inhabitant to produce more efficiently *and* to consume more intensively. Both were necessary to maintain a 'healthy growth rate'. The idea is simple and, as far as I know, uncontroversial. It is actually reminiscent of the sociologist Daniel Bell's famous dictum in a slightly later book, *The Cultural Contradictions of Capitalism*, according to which capitalism contradicts itself through a combination of a puritan work ethic and a hedonistic ethic of consumption. Linder nevertheless makes some original inferences which are relevant for the issues at hand. A high level of consumption is necessary to stimulate production, and increased production is necessary to reach the overarching goal of economic growth. As a result it becomes necessary, he says, to consume more and more in less and less time. Leisure time is increasingly turned into a mad rush for intensified consumption.

It is clear that Linder, who wrote with a particular view to tendencies in the USA of the 1960s, was far-sighted in this respect. In remote, underpopulated Norway, the large suburban shopping malls surrounded by enormous tarmac deserts arrived only in the 1980s. Here, one may park the car on a Saturday morning and spend a few hours consuming efficiently and intensively; much more so than in the old days, when shops were scattered and slow, dependent as they were on paying personal, individual attention to customers' needs. A couple of decades later, e-commerce contributes further to increasing efficiency of consumption.

Leisure time begins to resemble the work situation I described at the outset of this chapter. The turnover in CDs, books and clothes takes place at an accelerating pace. A major Norwegian book club, basing its profits on the negative option concept linked with a selection of the month, recently introduced its eighteenth book of the month in one year (without informing the members, most of whom probably never noticed). People stay fit through intensive programmes in health studios instead of travelling to more natural surroundings, and ready-made dishes to be heated in the microwave oven, making it possible to eat while watching television, have become common in most rich countries. In Norway, incidentally, the most popular dinner by far is the frozen pizza. The principle of stacking, described at length in the previous chapter, implies that there is less time available for each activity. The most obvious alternative for most of us would then consist in (1) reducing the time used for each activity, and/or (2) doing several things simultaneously. (I have several times been caught red-handed clicking with my computer mouse while talking on the phone, by perceptive conversation partners who recognised the sound.) No matter which alternative one chooses, there is less slow, continuous time left. And the marginal value continues to decrease. An information snippet worth 15 seconds of someone's attention in 1995, may not be valued at more than 5 seconds today. The producers chase the 'market' and cut, abbreviate, compress and tailor.

Time can always be economised a little bit more. Even a highly efficient consumer, who spends the evening zapping in front of the box while at the same time leafing through the paper, sending SMS messages, drinking beer, crunching crisps and smoking a low-tar cigarette, can no doubt become even more efficient. The boundary has not yet been reached. It is still easily possible to consume more during the day; the challenge (to the production side of the economy) consists in finding ways to make it happen. To citizens (who are not merely consumers), the goal may ultimately be the direct opposite.

The point is not that each activity changes that much, seen in isolation. There can be no doubt that the selection of crisp varieties has grown enormously, in accordance with the logic of stacking described in an earlier chapter: back in the dim and remote 1970s, there were in my country three varieties generally available: original, cheese and onion, and paprika. Today, the selection has grown many times over, and the traditional types are thus marketed as 'classic'. In spite of this impressive diversification in the crisp market, today's niche-oriented and consumer-adapted crisps are presumably eaten pretty much in the same way as that bag of cheese and onion crisps one was munching in the old days without doing anything else (except, perhaps, attempting to look one's spotty teenage girlfriend deep in the eyes between munches), but the act is surrounded by an entirely different semantic universe, crowded by competing signs.

Put differently: from 1993 to 2001, I was editor of a cultural journal that had existed for no less than 103 years when I took it over, called *Samtiden* (Norwegian for 'Contemporary times'). In spite of many facelifts and thematic shifts over the years, it remains today essentially the same journal as the one started by the professor and essayist Gerhard Gran in 1890. Like other cultural journals worthy of the label, it contains a varied menu of interviews, review essays, articles, polemics, analytical journalism, popular science and so on, delving into topics such as biology and culture, nationalism and multi-ethnic society, literature and human rights, new technology and its side-effects, ecology and moral philosophy. As late as the 1970s, the number of journals was so modest in Scandinavia, and the public sphere so easily surveyable, that a reading person could rightly feel that he or she kept apace with current issues and concerns by following two or three general-purpose journals (newspapers are generally dreadful in Norway, hence the importance of the cultural journals). Today, it is sufficient just to a glance at the journal racks of a well-stocked newsagent – one does not even have to venture into the Internet – to understand that the contemporary situation is completely different. The circulation of *Samtiden* is neither much higher nor much lower than it was in the past, but it is part of a very different informational ecology than before. A single journal can no longer suppose that it sets the agenda in a shared public sphere, but has to reconcile itself with sharing the stage, and the attention of the readers, with many others, all of which are shouting at the top of their voices. Each particular publication, be it a newspaper, a journal or a book, becomes neither less nor more than a fragment, a little speck in the grand mosaic, a colourful building block in an endless Legoland of information. This is all in all marvellous, it showcases the democratic and pluralistic dimensions of the present age. And yet...

The fragmentation of work, consumption, family life and the public sphere brings us to a world beyond ready-made 'identity packages'. Each must create their own coherent totality out of the disjointed fragments. A far from irrelevant question is whether such a task is at all manageable, or whether life is inevitably becoming more collage-like and filled with singular events and impressions, arbitrariness and spontaneity, short-term choices rather than some over-arching direction – that is, of a hegemonic fast mode rather than a mix between fast and slow modes. Many hold the view that this is exactly what happens in a lot of areas, from work to ethics, and commonly, the suggested shift is described as a transition from modernity to postmodernity. The influential sociologist Zygmunt Bauman named one of his recent books *Life in Fragments*, and he is far from alone in publishing books with this kind of title. Information society has already been proven to imply a whole range of unintended consequences, and one of the most important may tentatively be summed up as fragmentation, the dividing of time into ever decreasing units, and the ensuing loss of internal coherence. Symptoms of this effect could be anything from fundamentalism (voluntary exclusion of the world's infinite complexity) to extreme opportunism or burn-outs in professional life. Politics devoid of vision is another symptom, perhaps the most discouraging of all.

DOES THE INFORMATION REVOLUTION ACTUALLY INCREASE EFFICIENCY?

Before moving to a consideration of what can be done to mitigate the adverse effects of acceleration and stacking, I shall call attention to a final possible side-effect of the information revolution. For want of other, loftier aims, technologically driven changes within research, education and business enterprises are defended with reference to increased efficiency. But can we be certain that the streamlining of information management and the massive implementation of computerised routines do lead to increased efficiency? There are three possible answers:

(1) Yes, and it is great, because increased efficiency leads to economic growth.
(2) Yes, but it is worrying, since the extreme fetishisation of efficiency makes us forget real values.
(3) Actually no, paradoxically there is a tendency for technology that should presumably increase efficiency to work in an exact opposite way.

Option (3) is the most interesting one and the one I shall explore, although naturally a lot could also be said about the relationship between (1) and (2) as well. Suppose this was the most fundamental side-effect of the information revolution? That it does not even increase efficiency? Several unintended consequences of technological change have already been discussed in this book, and they are

frequently easy to see. It does not, for example, require a lot of imagination to understand that the introduction of that male potency
technology called Viagra would lead to increased demand for pros-
titutes all over the world. A little less obvious is the fact that the
telefax came into common use in Europe a long time after its
invention; primitive faxes had actually existed almost as long as the
telegraph. It happened during a major postal strike in Britain during
the mid-1980s.

A more subtle kind of side-effect is the one Paul Virilio calls
attention to when he speaks of 'grey ecology', that is *the pollution of
space*. When the jet plane replaced the passenger ship as the means
of transportation from Europe to the USA, he points out, the Atlantic
Ocean ceased to exist. In order to discover side-effects of this kind,
a historical frame of mind is required: one must remember or learn
what it used to be like. This is one of the most daunting tasks faced
by people subjected to the tyranny of the moment. It is primarily in
this sense that the loss of a sense of history is dangerous.

Many side-effects are associated with information technology. So-
called time-managers (including Filofaxes) are constructed in such a
way that most users will need a lot of time to find out how to utilise
them rationally. As is well known, courses are offered to teach people
how to distinguish between their different levels and entry systems.
With advanced computer programs, the situation is comparable and
often worse. They stimulate the user to dive deeply into the
mysteries of the programs themselves, instead of simply using them
to do their job, and are sent on costly courses just to learn their functioning. (And when the user is finally conversant with the software,
it is replaced by the next generation of applications.) Mobile
telephony and e-mail also have curious side-effects. Both of these
technologies render the user more mobile and flexible than before;
one can send and reply to messages anytime, anywhere. These technologies seem, in other words, to liberate time, making the users
flexible and in greater command of their own time budgets.
However, as indicated indirectly in the previous chapters, the
outcome has been the exact opposite. E-mail and mobile telephony
creates a kind of flexibility entailing that one is expected to be
accessible at any time. One is, in a sense, never properly out of the
office. Suppose I have been physically out of the office for a day; I
return, turn on the computer, and receive an avalanche of e-mails.
Several of them end on the ominous note: 'Call me before 1:30 this
afternoon.' Furthermore, those valuable gaps that occur as one drives

or takes the tube to work, are suddenly gone. One is reachable, and is able to work, while standing at a bus stop. These spaces are being polluted in the same way as the Sargasso Sea.

When there is only a little e-mail and few calls, such technologies are doubtless liberating. When the number of incoming messages exceeds a certain threshold, the functioning of the very same technologies suddenly flips into its opposite. They begin to imprison the users, fill the gaps and kill those empty, slow periods that are so important for creativity and directionless thinking. Enthusiastic supporters of the private car worship it for making it possible to move fast and without delay at any time. But when the number of cars becomes so great that the average speed drops down to that of a bicycle (while children and adults alike collapse due to respiratory diseases), even the most enthusiastic driver might seriously consider converting to tram or bicycle. It should be no different in the case of the new information technologies.

Hardly anyone had expected time to move faster and become more scarce as a result of introducing time-saving technology. This is nevertheless just what has happened. In this insight lies, perhaps, the germ of an answer to the question raised at the end of Chapter 5, namely how it can be that exponential growth curves sooner or later flatten out.

It is far from everything that moves faster and faster, even within the general framework of the technologies of acceleration. Air travel is an obvious example: about half of the flights connecting major European cities are currently delayed. The sky over the London–Milan axis is heavily congested. The most famous example is still the close cousin of air traffic, namely road traffic. It grows quickly – between 1970 and 2000 it trebled in the home of the car, that is the USA – but although billions are spent on highways, flyovers and turnpikes, speed decreases year by year. The average speed for a moving car in Manhattan is now 11 kilometres per hour. There are other major cities which are even worse off. Take Bangkok, for example, where some have installed *lavatories* in their cars as a consequence of spending a large part of their day in rush hour queues. It is estimated that 2.3 million person hours were lost in traffic delays in Los Angeles in 1994. The highways become wider, but in mysterious ways they continue to be filled up. For several hours every day they look more like giant car parks than super-efficient transport arteries. The average driver in Washington, DC loses 71 hours a year in traffic jams.

The average number of minutes used waiting to get through on the telephone is probably also pretty high, and, although I have not found statistics in the field, it is likely to have grown considerably, given the enormous growth of speech telephony. It would be interesting to know how many man-labour years were lost annually through the 'please hold' syndrome. Or how many lazy afternoons on the terrace, football games with the kids, novel readings or walks in the sun, for that matter.

A related example is this: a new railway tunnel connects Oslo with the small satellite town Lillestrøm. When it was finally opened in August 1999, following an incredible series of budgetary and other scandals, the tunnel reduced the travel time on the stretch with 14 minutes. The stretch is part of the new airport railway leading from Oslo to its new airport at Gardermoen, 55 kilometres north of the city. There was a train connection before – the important railway from Oslo to Trondheim went past Gardermoen – but the stretch was improved at a cost of 10 billion kroner (£800 million), 90 per cent of which was pure loss. If all kinds of time, including travel time, can be measured in money, it may still be possible to calculate that this investment was worthwhile and will eventually pay off. Nevertheless, I have my doubts, and not just because the budget deficit on the Gardermoen railway is equal to the total expected ticket sales for the next 31 years. It is obvious that great chunks of those 14 saved minutes are immediately eaten up; waiting in queues at the airport or simply waiting for a delayed flight, waiting for the tube or tram, while the taxi is waiting at traffic lights and so on. The extremely fast time connecting Lillestrøm with Oslo is quickly consumed by the slow and less controllable time characteristics of the surrounding links.

The flight time itself between Oslo and other European cities is so short that one is tempted to believe that Copenhagen is only 45 minutes away, London an hour and a half. But then there is all the preparatory and 'postparatory' activity, the queues at check-in, security and immigration; the waiting to have a time slot allocated when there is much traffic in the air. The ride on the Piccadilly line into town (which could take nearly as long as the flight from Oslo), or the excruciating drive into town by taxi. The extra margin one has to allow when leaving home, and so on. *Impatience*, that characteristic side-effect of the tyranny of the moment, is a function of sudden shifts between fast and slow modes.

In addition, it cannot be taken for granted that all travel time can be meaningfully measured in money. The train is nowadays presented as a quiet alternative to the plane and the car; the train – the very symbol of speed and efficiency in Victorian times – is now a site of contemplation, a place where one may seek inner peace, read a book chapter, drink a cup of coffee, and ruminate over the curious aspects of life while gazing at the passing countryside.

At the same time, speed threatens to dominate even such enforced slow contexts. Information technology helps to fill the gaps. The growing market for portable computers and PDAs (palmtops) is directly connected to the amount of time people spend waiting at airports, and it would surprise me if there were not a connection between rush traffic and the spread of the mobile phone. In the Scandinavian countries, the combination driving/talking on the phone is so common that legislation has been passed which makes it mandatory to use handsfree accessories when talking on the phone in the car. A number of local trains are now equipped with TV monitors, and several, including the new airport express train from Arlanda airport to Stockholm city, use them to send current news and weather forecasts. Whether one becomes more efficient by filling the gaps in this way, is another question. More and more people concede that, in order to get something substantial done, they have to get out of the office and work at home or even in a remote cabin.

The unintended consequences of computer use are so many that they would deserve an entire book. Some have already been mentioned; here is another: to anyone who writes, continuous concentration is an indispensable asset. What counts when a writing person chooses a computer, is really just the keyboard and the monitor. My first computers were primitive creations (the trilobites of personal computing), where it was only possible to access one application at the time. In other words, they made it necessary to write when one was supposed to do so. If one were distracted by unwelcome intrusions from the outside world, that was not the computer's fault. Today, the writer's gaze flicks between Eudora, Netscape, the electronic diary and the word processor; in many cases games and music as well. Every moment is being disturbed by the next. The best word processing machine that was ever made, may have been the Macintosh SE, which existed from 1987 to 1990. The monitor was small and in black and white, but sharp. The keyboard was comfortable. The hard disk had space for a nearly unlimited number of articles and treatises, but not for a lot of other things. The memory was modest, and for a long time it was impossible to keep more than one application open at the time. Personally, I have never since written in a similarly concentrated mode as during those years in the early 1990s when I was working on this kind of computer.

It is necessary to understand these side-effects of technology, not in order to relegate computers and mobile phones to the scrapyard of history (the Luddite mistake), but in order to be able to use them in sensible ways. As the next chapter will make clear, a proper understanding of the structural forces shaping our situation helps, but it is far from enough. Good intentions are free and lead, in themselves, to nothing.

8   The Pleasures of Slow Time

> There is only one thing that is worse than being short of time.
> That is not being short of time.
>
> (T.H.E., with apologies to Oscar Wilde)

Mister Figaro was a hairdresser in a remote town. He enjoyed his work and his friends, he played music, looked after his old mother and paid a chronically ill woman a visit every afternoon. Yet he often felt empty and sad. One day he got a call from a man who offered a recipe for a better life. The man, dressed in grey from top to toe and smoking a small grey cigar, represented the Time Savings Bank. He showed Figaro how he could save time in order to become a happier person. Place your mother in an institution for the elderly, stop visiting that useless invalid, stop wasting precious time chatting with your customers – then you will double your turnover – and 'above all, don't squander so much of your precious time on singing, reading and hobnobbing with your so-called friends'.

Figaro followed the advice. He became taciturn and efficient. And yet: 'No matter how much time he saved, he never had any to spare; in some mysterious way, it simply vanished. (...) Almost before he knew it, another week had gone by, and another month, and another year, and another and another.'

The hairdresser was not the only victim of the grey functionaries of the Time Savings Bank. The whole town seemed to have opened accounts with them. Slogans such as 'Get more out of life – save time!' appeared on the walls, and notices that were placed in factories and office buildings might read, 'Time is precious – don't waste it!' or even 'Time is money – save it!'

The end of the story I shall refrain from revealing; the reader might instead take an afternoon off to read Michael Ende's little novel *Momo*. It is time well spent, that much I promise.

The most obvious objection to my analysis so far goes like this: 'Most people do not have this experience of their life. They lead their lives in peace and quiet, they do not run incessantly from web pages to e-mail to heaps of documents to meetings to rush-hour queues to deadlines. They do not feel a constant pressure to be flexible, open and youthful. They have plenty of time to sit down in an easy chair with a pipe and a novel, or they take leisurely walks in the country, and are able to enjoy life at their own pace. The people you write about belong to a small minority, don't pretend otherwise!'

Point taken. But does this then mean that a majority of the inhabitants of rich countries never watch television, never talk over the mobile phone or write e-mail, never read tabloids, have never applied for a job where familiarity with IT is an essential requirement, and never feel that they do not have enough time for things that really matter because there is always something else they have to do first? And never feel that they cannot concentrate properly on whatever they are doing because new urgent tasks are waiting?

It is obvious that the side-effects of the information age affect people to varying degrees. Not everybody has the feeling that time is accelerating. Quite a few people, even in the most fast-moving societies in the world, have the experience that *fast time is a scarce resource*. Take unemployed people, for example. Or prison inmates. Or the impoverished and marginalised millions of people in North American urban slums. This has to be taken into account. Yet, I would, on the basis of the previous chapters, state categorically that:

(1) A fragmented and rushed temporality is typical of a growing majority of the population in the rich countries.
(2) Acceleration affects both the production of knowledge and the very mode of thought in contemporary culture, and therefore concerns everybody. Even an unemployed person with aeons of 'time to kill', is sucked up by the side-effects of acceleration the moment he or she turns on the TV or opens the newspaper.

Obviously this situation, where both working time and leisure time are cut into pieces, where the intervals become smaller and smaller, where a growing number of events are squeezed into decreasing time slots, is not arrived at by general consensus in the population. Even the most powerful people, who might be expected to be in control of their own time, complain (generally more than anybody else) that their tight schedules preclude evenings in the theatre, reading novels and so on. They are just as much slaves of the clock as anybody else. The son of a former Norwegian prime minister, the academic Henrik Syse, told the press recently that he saw a political career as impossible to reconcile with a functioning family life, because 'the pressure created by piles of documents and meetings is much tougher nowadays than it used to be'.

Before moving towards some recommendations, I shall sum up the main points developed in this book.

- *When there is a surplus, and no scarcity, of information, the degree of comprehension falls in proportion with the growth in amount of information.* One has to limit one's information out of consideration for one's knowledge. Often, students write their best papers about the topics they are least familiar with; this forces them to structure, justify and argue better than they usually do, and the main argument does not drown in details and digressions. Put differently: after spending six months in a foreign country, you can write a book. After ten years, you can write an article. The more you know, the more you do not know. This general principle is part of the human condition in information society. We know more and more, and therefore we know less and less.

- *The main scarce resource for suppliers of any commodity in the information society is the attention of others.* Whether it is advertisements, talks, scientific articles, knowledge or simply physical commodities that we offer the outside world, there is an intensified competition for the vacant slots in the time budgets of the target groups. These vacant moments become fewer and shorter, since the people in question are subjected to powerful expectations that they should squeeze ever more impressions, commodities, experiences and pieces of information into their lives. The next impression kills the previous one at an accelerating speed.

- *The main scarce resource for inhabitants of the information society is well-functioning filters.* This point is identical with the previous point, differing only in that it sees the situation from the recipient's perspective. E-mail is a blessing for senders, a nightmare for receivers. If one receives more e-letters than one sends, it may indicate that one is not in charge of one's total flow of information. We are short of commodities that our grandparents had never heard of; one typical scarce resource today is lack of information.

- *Acceleration removes distance, space and time.* This was once the main criticism against the steam train – the passengers lose the ability to enjoy the landscape, and their mind becomes hurried in an unhealthy way. Today, the criticism is levelled against the jet plane, the Internet and mobile telecommunications. When that which used to be remote no longer is remote, that which used to be near is no longer near either.

- *When fast and slow time meet, fast time wins.* This is why one never gets the important things done because there is always something else one has to do first. Naturally, we will always tend to do the most urgent tasks first. In this way, the slow and long-term activities lose out. In an age when the distinctions between work and leisure are being erased, and efficiency seems to be the only value in economics, politics and research, this is really bad news for things like thorough, far-sighted work, play and long-term love relationships.

- *Flexible work creates a loss of flexibility in the non-work areas of life.* This is because of the general tendency for fast time to conquer slow time. If flexibility is defined as unexploited potential, jobs that potentially fill every gap remove flexibility elsewhere, with serious consequences, affecting creativity, family life and people's mental well-being.

- *When time is partitioned into sufficiently small pieces, it eventually ceases to exist as duration.* All that is ultimately left, is a screaming, packed moment which stands still at a frightful speed.

Entirely negative criticism can only lead to shrugs alternating with anxiety. For this reason, some positive suggestions are necessary, and to them we now move. I shall nevertheless first make a leisurely detour to the ivory tower of academia, since we still have plenty of time.

Many are worried about the state of things. Indeed, a sizeable number of intellectuals are even paid by the state to keep such worries going (the *raison-d'être* of the social sciences: generalised anxiety). Some of them adopt a sarcastic and condescending tone of voice when they address colleagues who are not sufficiently worried. Lately, some of the victims of this internal policing have been the sociologists Anthony Giddens (adviser to Tony Blair) and Manuel Castells (specialist on the global techno-economy).

Interestingly, the laments of influential academic worriers have changed during the past couple of decades. Until the late 1970s or early 1980s, most of them were chiefly concerned with the oppression caused by capitalist production, the exploitation of the working class and neo-imperialism in the Third World; sub-groups directed their considerable worrying power towards the nuclear threat and/or global population growth, patriarchy and environmental problems. Lately, the centre of gravity of the academic anxiety industry has moved towards questions to do with identity and – I would argue – an accelerated rate of change. One of the ex-Marxist Giddens's latest books is called *Runaway World* and is to do with the identity aspect of globalisation; a very promising growth industry among American academic worriers has been globalisation and identity in multicultural societies (or post-multi-ethnic society, a concept generated by conventional academic one-upmanship); sociologists like Zygmunt Bauman and Ulrich Beck have become figureheads for their work on risk, uncertainty, ambivalence and – more generally – difficulties of developing a cohesive, trustworthy world-view in this turbulent era. Some of the most influential French intellectuals see the lack of coherence and overview as a particularly important threat to democracy and liberating values – Bourdieu seems to have changed his priorities in this direction, and Paul Virilio, who has written about the theory of speed for thirty years, has recently entered the Premier Division of French thinkers, and his reputation in the USA (a certain indication of academic rank) is growing. In Italy, Umberto Eco represents a similar position, which is also amply represented in Germany and the USA. The point is that the phenomena I have grouped under the sub-headings acceleration, exponential growth and stacking – the tyranny of the moment – are now taken deadly seriously by a great number of scholars who otherwise have little in common. Their topics are both wide and narrow – some write about the new, opaque global economy, others about the vulnerability created by new technology, and yet others about the confusing effects of flickering news.

The current diagnoses represented in the discrete analyses of many very different thinkers, have much in common. Tellingly, few of them has a word to say about what ought to be done. Castells ends his three-volume work on the information age with a cautious warning against building castles in the air as was common when he was a young man (that is, in the mythical 1960s, which chronologically largely took place in the 1970s). Giddens talks eloquently and fluently about a new democratic order (of 'dialogic democracy') where everybody should supposedly be represented, but tangible substance has not exactly been the trademark of his writings from the last decade – important as they may still be in other ways.

Bourdieu is deeply pessimistic. He seems to propose turning to the 'Off' button, while Baudrillard escapes through dark humour and Virilio earnestly declares that he does not see a solution to the problems caused by acceleration and information overload.

To non-academic readers, it may seem odd that so many sharp thinkers take such an anaemic and impotent stance towards a family of problems which, in their view, is overwhelmingly important in our culture. It may be that the main reason is their position in society, as carriers of enlightenment, *Bildung*: slow, linear, cumulative, cohesive knowledge. They belong to an obscure minority of bourgeois intellectuals who, in the old days, had oceans of leisurely time to think and read, and to write heavy, voluminous and often unnecessarily complicated texts for readers who had plenty of time to spare, a good dictionary and considerable fear of authority. Their time is probably gone, never to return in its original form. Habermas prophesied that much already in 1961, in his *Strukturwandeln der Öffentlichkeit* (*The Structural Transformation of the Public Sphere*). Nowadays, it is only masochists who can feel gratitude welling up as they are presented with thick, dense and dry academic texts. There is too much, not too little information. Whatever can be communicated fast, should thus be communicated fast. Adhering to this principle attests to respect for one's readers. Only those who are bringers of unusually important, necessarily slow and complicated insights, have the right to claim weeks of their readers' time. Others should keep in mind that whatever it is that they write competes with other sources of information. This is one of several causes for the declining social (and economic) rank of academic intellectuals in recent years. We must find our place in the new ecology of information, and the first step must consist in proposing viable solutions to the side-effects of acceleration.

Everything that can be done quickly, threatens to do away with everything that must be done slowly. As a result, slow processes are transmuted into fast ones. The fully deserved world success of Jostein Gaarder's *Sophie's World* in the mid-1990s can obviously be traced to such a transmutation. The history of philosophy in its old shape had a snowball's chance in hell of surviving as an element in the personality formation of the majority. It was too heavy, slow, time-consuming and boring. Enter a mildly entertaining and cunningly composed novel for adolescents, which whirls through the high points of 2,500 years of philosophy without the engaged reader even noticing it. In this way it becomes possible, even for people who are otherwise hemmed in by unanswered e-mail, soap operas, packed meeting schedules and rush-hour traffic jams, to grab – between collecting in kindergarten and that evening meeting in the project group – some juicy mouthfuls about this Aristotle gentleman and that Hegel foghead. And what is wrong with that? Fast food is incomparably better than no food. Whenever I travel by plane, as mentioned earlier, I drink a kind of coffee I would otherwise categorise as undrinkable, which carries the prefix instant. Simply because it is the only coffee available.

There are three kinds of answers to this kind of problem. First, academics who, as a matter of principle, would prefer that everybody strives to be like themselves, would most likely hold that instant coffee and popularised philosophy are worse than nothing. Rather illiteracy than the *Sun*; *Die Welt* or nothing.

A second response would claim that anything is better than nothing. This is a point of view which fits current sensibilities well, which seems open-minded and generous, and which clearly has a wider appeal than the other view. You can eat your cake and have it, you can have an immensely rich life, and you will have time for everything if you try hard enough. Optimism is a fine quality, but it does not always lead to the best description of reality. It may well be that, confronted with the choice of skimming ten books or reading one of them properly, one will be best rewarded by the last alternative. (One must only make certain that one chooses the right one. No wonder ambivalence is one of the defining sentiments of our time!)

The third kind of attitude entails that increased efficiency is always for the better. There exist a considerable number of unreformed optimists who do not think that the loss of slow time will have any consequences other than making it possible for us to do more than earlier generations were able to. Peter Cochrane, research director at British Telecom, has declared that he already thinks of the computer as 'my third brain hemisphere': 'My father had a working life of 100,000 hours. I could do everything he did in 10,000 hours and my son will be able to do it in 1,000.' But would the *content* of the work still remain the same? Obviously not, but if the entire culture is based on extreme speed and particular, agreed-upon ways of measuring efficiency, and the opposition disappears into the dark holes of academia and high culture because it is unable to catch up, then it is in no way certain that a lot of people would notice the difference.

In spite of the optimism represented in the view of Cochrane and others, the distinction between fast and slow time is still meaningful to many of us; and, although both may be necessary in a modern (or postmodern) society, it is difficult to defend the view that speed and efficiency are scarce. My own position, incidentally, is conveniently wedged in the gap between the first and second alternatives, and it is the only sound position.

The recommendations that follow below presuppose that it is slowness, not speed, that is threatened. (Anyone not in agreement with this, may send me an e-mail... no, send me a letter, preferably handwritten.) I begin with some suggestions aimed at the personal level – what you and I can do – followed by a few challenges thrown in the general direction of politicians and business leaders.

What can be done quickly, should be done quickly. Fast time is splendid when it is used appropriately (but a dangerous tool in the hands of the unskilled). Never before in history have as many people had the opportunity to take in as many impressions and experiences as today. When critics abhor these opportunities (ranging from the growth of tourism to the mushrooming of Internet connections), they entirely disregard the fact that exhilarating computer games, exciting, event-packed holidays in remote places, aimless zapping or short newsreels may be deeply valued by the users, and are probably better than nothing (which is often the alternative).

Some things move fast, others move slowly. Nobody watches the second hand during a romantic dinner. Even in heavy theoretical work, there are insights that come quickly and others that can only be developed over years. A logician may peak in his career before he is 30, while few metaphysicians have published anything of lasting value before their fifties. The greatest social anthropological thinker of the twentieth century, Claude Lévi-Strauss, took quite a long time. Before he published a book that revolutionised our thinking about kinship in 1949, he had spent four years reflecting on issues like 'How can it be that the Indian caste system seems to be a mirror-inversion of Australian kinship systems?' Had he been funded by a major research council in the late 1990s, he would have lost his grant long before completing his work, due to lack of documented progress. Everything has its cost, and efficiency in the production of knowledge may imply both death and salvation, depending on the kind of knowledge one searches for.

A lot of things can be done fast in good conscience, especially routine things. Some kinds of consumption are also tailored to be carried out fast; there is relatively little to be gained by slow, careful listening to pop singles or slow savouring of hamburgers from a global chain. Conversely, Proust and Mahler offer naught to a consumer who tries to apply methods taken from the consumption of Stephen King or Britney Spears to their work.

A lot of what we do are hybrid activities that mix speed with slowness. An experienced lecturer may well say, therefore, that the preparations for a particular lecture has taken her somewhere between 10 minutes and 30 years. Moreover, there are activities we usually associate with speed (or desired speed), that could profitably be redefined as slow ones, commuting, for example. (Obvious advice: bring a paperback.) Those who read or listen to music are less susceptible to ulcers than those who stare stiffly at the bus schedules.

Slow time is not the same thing as a great amount of time. It takes only a few minutes to read and understand a poem of average complexity, but it has to be done slowly. Speed reading is a blessed skill when one uses it to activate one's carefully honed filters in skimming large masses of text in search of a particular passage or fact (such as during a Web search), but those who instinctively look for the subject index when they get a new novel, are – naturally – already severely damaged.

Dawdling is a virtue as long as nobody gets hurt. In the chapter about speed, I wrote about acceleration in the nineteenth century, and spoke about – among other things – the telegraph, the steam train and Knut Hamsun's letters from America. In the initial plans for this book, I had no intention of paying so much attention to these examples. Some of them are included in their present form simply because, one morning in June 2000, I was suddenly given an hour of empty time. I had delivered a defective lamp to the shop and found myself in a part of Oslo which I rarely visit. Due to an administrative slip on my part, my first meeting was more than an hour off, and it was going to be in the same part of town. I do not have a WAP telephone, and I am not yet addicted to the mobile. Therefore, I strolled leisurely down the beautiful main street of the suburb (called Bygdøy Allé) in the sun, pensively licking a brightly coloured ice lolly. As I reached the main roundabout near the venue of my meeting, my eye caught an enormous banner covering a large part of the front of the old University Library. 'Speed 1800–1900', it said. Naturally I was drawn towards the building like a fly towards flypaper, and quite right: the library featured a small, but excellent exhibition about my topic, displaced about a hundred years back in history. Had I not been fooling around aimlessly that morning, I should never have even heard about the exhibition.

A few weeks later, I only had about 10 minutes to spare waiting for my tram, but I spent them in a large newsagent's near the National Theatre. After a couple of minutes of random scanning among the shelves, my gaze fell for a couple of continuous seconds on a new magazine about 'e-business'. Scandinavian technophiles are also Americophiles and tend to make their most pompous statements in US English, and so I was only surprised by the message (not by the linguistic medium) when I read, in enormous types: 'SURVIVAL OF THE FASCISTS', on the cover. I picked up the magazine. Had the IT business finally discovered other values than dollars and yen? On the tram, I began to read, and quickly discovered that my initial interpretation must have been a Freudian slip. The actual heading read: 'SURVIVAL OF THE FASTEST'. The feature story indicated that the turnover speed in the IT business now began to approach the limits of human tolerance. If anything, I returned to my computer reinforced in my belief that my choice of topic had been the correct one. Again, this snippet of encouragement would not have come my way unless I had been wasting time. *Creativity*, in other words, is directly produced by the gaps.

Slowness needs protection. It is an asylum-seeker whose tear-stained application is often turned down by the powers that be. It needs all the public support, social benefits, subsidies and quotas it can get. Speed manages perfectly well on its own, there is nothing more competitive than speed. Depending on one's personal and professional situation, one may on an individual level protect slowness in different ways; but it must be chosen consciously in order not to be eaten alive by speed. Such decisions may, for example, look like this:

- I respond to e-mail on Monday mornings only.
- Every Tuesday I am unavailable, since I am fishing at a secret place.
- I commute 60 miles every day. Driving to and from work, I am alone in the car, with the mobile phone and the radio turned off.
- On Tuesdays and Thursdays I read journals instead of newspapers.
- I have no answering machine. When I am not in, I am not in.
- Before I read the news on WAP, I always read a poem and two footnotes.
- Between 4.30 and 8.30 p.m. I am with my family, and am therefore not available for the outside world.

- I go to the Concert House every second Wednesday to listen to orchestral works without distractions or interruptions.
- I live in the present moment whenever it suits me, and refuse to be interrupted by the next moment.

Delays are blessings in disguise. They create gaps for afterthoughts, one just has to know how to exploit them. Easier said than done? Certainly, but every time one feels relief because a meeting has been postponed, one has begun to realise it.

The logic of the wood cabin deserves to be globalised. In the Scandinavian countries (including Finland in this respect), the notion of the cottage or cabin, *hytta* (N) or *stugan* (S) or *sommerhuset* (DK), has special connotations. Only about half of the Scandinavian population have easy access to such cottages, but everybody is aware of their deeper significance. When one arrives at the cottage, which is located either in a remote and barren place in the mountains or on a deserted strip of coastline (Denmark is an exception here, for obvious reasons), the temporality of slowness takes over. One puts the watch in a drawer, leaving it there until it is time to return to the city. Many families have violent discussions about whether to have TV, telephone and Internet connectivity in the cottage – although many do have these conveniences, they are ashamed to admit it. Many people, especially Norwegians, even refuse to have electricity in their cottages. In this context, it is not the pressure of the clock that regulates activities, but the activities that regulate the organisation of time. The children go to bed at a later hour than usual, dinner is served as a result of mounting hunger, berry picking and fishing last as long as one feels like it, and so on. The irony is that many people are fantastically prolific in such an environment, where the next moment is not looking over the shoulder of the present, asking it to step aside. (These lines are being written – you guessed it – in our cottage!) Now, very few citizens in modern societies dream of a permanent return to such a state of blissful peace. We know too much about other kinds of pleasures, and understand the complexities of our present society too well for that kind of regressive dream to be truly attractive. Yet we should not forget that the temporal regime of the cottage differs radically from that fragmented, rushed regime which regulates so much of our lives in general. I should think that cottage time could profitably be applied to a wide range of activities, if not to activities that by default need to be carefully and accurately coordinated. (In this area, it seems as if Northerners have a comparative advantage in handling the time tyranny: the closest equivalent in Britain seems to be cricket, and it is really not the same thing.)

All decisions exclude as much as they include. Long, profound news programmes and long periods in remote areas may be preferable to their short alternatives; the problem is only that everything one spends time on is parasitical on something else that one might also want to spend time on. And how can I be so certain that it is sensible time use to spend a semester reading Kant or staying in a slow-moving Thai fishing village, when I am overwhelmed by other, less demanding and less mutually excluding activities? If I have to prioritise, what criteria can I apply? For want of self-evident criteria, many try to find time for everything. As a result, each single event or activity suffers. That is exactly the problem.

Suppose you have spent money, taken unpaid leave from your job or studies, sent your children off to kind relations in the country, and have allowed yourself half a year earmarked for some truly fulfilling activity. Suppose, further, that the following activities are the first to come to mind:

- Learn to play jazz piano.
- Spend six months in Paris to learn French properly.
- Become really skilful at building virtual cities in the latest version of SimCity.
- Get acquainted with symbolic logic.
- Read *Ulysses*.
- Look after your family and become a better cook.
- Have a good time in cafés and cinemas with your friends.
- Spend as much time as possible in a hammock on a tropical beach.

All good and laudable intentions in their way, but all of them cannot, naturally, be implemented at the same time. Two or three alternatives may be combined, but a more packed schedule would ruin everything. It is in this light that the notion that our generation has the opportunity to experience 17 times as much as our great-grandparents, must be taken with a pinch of salt. The laws of diminishing returns and stacking apply with full force.

In an earlier chapter, I mentioned that certain people, with unusual capacities and energies, are able to do twelve things simultaneously and well. Then they get a thirteenth task, and suddenly they do thirteen things badly, or else they collapse and drift away on sick leave based on diffuse symptoms. This insight is a more fruitful starting-point than any pessimistic or neo-Luddite suggestion about using the 'Off' button. Speed is a great gift until it gets out of hand. Like thousands of other anthropologists, I have lived in a tropical village during fieldwork. Everyday life in the village was not exactly wanting in slowness. *Time* was, to most of the inhabitants, not a measurable, scarce resource. Life rolled on at a leisurely rhythm. After a few months, naturally, I was bored out of my wits. Interestingly, this was also the case with many of the villagers, particularly the young men and women. They had, it seemed, been waiting for life to speed up since they were born, living as they did on the fringes of modernity, exposed to fast-moving films and stories from big cities.

There is no need, in other words, to romanticise limitless slowness. Modernity *is* speed. At the moment, however, it is going too fast, a fact which is a main connotation of Umberto Eco's term 'hypermodernity'.

It is necessary to switch consciously between fast and slow time. Restlessness is a personal quality which thrives these days. Generally, this state of mind arises when slow time meets an expectation of fast time. Rush-hour traffic and delayed flights are paradigmatic examples. In an old article from *Der Spiegel* (from 1989, to be accurate), a 9-year-old is quoted as saying: 'My teachers talk more slowly than my Atari, so slowly that it sometimes drives me crazy. I think: Come on, that will do. Let me go home to my Atari. It is able to tell me things more quickly.'

However, a 5-year-old who was interviewed in a UN study about education for small children, stated in 1999: 'I never get to play. Always, it is just "Hurry up! Hurry up!" I hate hurrying up.' Together, these two quotations reveal that both opposing (or complementary) tendencies exist side by side: a restlessness caused by the slowness of others, and frustration over external demands for speed and efficiency.

The difference between the two statements naturally consists in the fact that the German 9-year-old (who is already a university student by now) regulates his own speed at the keyboard, while the tempo of the 5-year-old is entirely directed from outside. The solution consists in taking conscious charge of one's own rhythmic changes.

Most things one will never need to know about. Some of us would be better off saying to ourselves, perhaps several times a day, that people are up to a lot of funny things; most of it you do not have to know about, even if it might be great stuff. What matters more than anything else in this context, is to equip oneself with sturdy, efficient filters which consist of taste, values, interests and intuition. They, incidentally, can only be acquired slowly.

Slowness needs much more than this kind of personal training programme in order to survive; it needs support from the state, trade unions and employers' organisations, politicians and NGOs – it must be embedded in the structure of society. It is far from sufficient to appeal to the good intentions of every individual. Good intentions are free and uncommitting, and are sooner or later caught up with by the system. It is easy, and not least free, to raise one's index finger to state that now we'd better spend more time offline, watch less stupid television and read good old-fashioned journals instead, stop writing so much e-mail and turn off the mobile phone, travel by train rather than by plane and give ourselves ample time whenever we are with children or elderly people. Even if certain admonitions of this kind may have a slightly higher value than the cost of the print run, they are clearly limited. If it is going to be at all possible to limit the side-effects of information society, societal priorities are required. If would help significantly if politicians, bureaucrats and business leaders realised that currently we have a golden chance to get the best from both worlds – the fast and the slow – and that immeasurable values are lost if we end up only seeing one of them.

Just as the nineteenth-century working class had to fight patiently and militantly to make industrialism serve some of their ends (and not just those of the capitalists), the struggle over our era's scarce resource – slowness – is going to lead to major confrontations. Probably, in this struggle, technocrats (including many social democrats) and big money will be on the wrong side; they share an almost religious belief in efficiency as a value in itself.

The tyranny of the moment can only be resisted efficiently if society introduces *brakes* as an integral element in its structure.

How?

A major portion of this book has dealt with unintended consequences or side-effects of change. In some cases, the side-effects are so considerable that losses and gains equal each other out. A standard example is car traffic in the densest urban areas in the world. Let traffic problems serve as a metaphoric starting-point for a look at information problems. The marginal value of driving falls towards zero when the bicycle becomes a faster means of transportation. The marginal value of information acquisition falls towards zero when the user becomes more confused and not better informed (or more entertained) by the waves of information. The marginal value of living in the here and now falls towards zero when the succession of moments is so swift that people are more concerned with the next moment than with the present one.

The traffic jam literally puts brakes on driving, but it has to be conceded that so far, this, has not made a lot of people convert to cycling. It may also be the case that the cacophony of information does not discourage people, but on the contrary leads to addiction. A constant flow input of impressions and decontextualised fragments thus becomes virtually a bodily need. This is a possibility not to be disregarded. Over the coming years, both broadband and digital TV will become widespread, and omnipresent, wireless information technologies such as the Bluetooth chip – a 'command centre of digital communication' fusing several known technologies into a seamless system – may also make a major impact in rich, technophile countries from Scandinavia to the USA. State restrictions on bandwidth and net access is a strategy that properly belongs to old-fashioned totalitarian regimes. Suppose, then, that the mass media instead established an internal set of guidelines to regulate the relationship between slowness and speed? Let this, therefore, be my first proposal at the societal level:

Ethical guidelines for the press should be extended to include a set of rules regarding slowness. In most European countries, press organisations have established more or less efficient norms regulating other ethical principles, and such an extension would simply build on existing frameworks in each country. Material which by its nature demands slowness (e.g. major tragedies, science news, details about the national budget) should be transmitted slowly, no matter the medium. It would be a breach of the rules if, say, genetic research was dealt with in the same form as the latest news from the world of pop music. Sanctions would apply.

The next proposal is also directly linked to the production of knowledge, and is to do with the unfortunate side-effects of stacking. In sum, too much text is being produced, at least in the rich countries. It may be the case that the total sum of happiness in a given society grows as it increases its production of vacuum cleaners and toasters, but the relationship between quantity and quality is a complex one, and nowhere is this more evident than in the field of information. The proposal goes like this:

The principle of 'less is more' should be established as a norm among suppliers of information. If article A is twice as long as article B, it should also be twice as complex. Prolific writers on a monthly salary should be offered incentives to reduce their productivity, in so far as it implies improved quality. For example, established professors who write a lot might be encouraged to keep quiet for five years, provided they then came up with a piece that made a difference. (An acquaintance of mine once suggested that all writers should have a maximum quota of 500 pages. If they exceeded that limit, they would have to withdraw some of their earlier work.) This would entail a need to evaluate quality rather than simply counting number of publications.

The next proposals deal with e-mail and mobile telecommunications. Only a minority long for that technological stone age when we had hardly heard about any of these, but we also have the right to live in a society where both kinds of technology (which are about to merge) are genuinely useful. Being unavailable is, as is well known, a very scarce resource in an increasingly wired world.

All employees should have the right to be offline for one month a year outside of vacations. This right should be embedded in the labour contract, where it should also be stated that nobody is obliged to respond to e-mail outside office hours. Office computers should have the following message engraved on the monitor: 'Send e-mail only when you have to.'

Public spaces – restaurants, banks, buses, lifts – should be mobile-free zones. This can easily be implemented by mounting noise transmitters in discreet places (in a sense, this represents the opposite of closed-circuit video monitoring – people are delinked instead of being under surveillance). In cases of emergency, as when the tube stops for two hours between stations, the noise transmitters may be turned off. An additional suggestion could be that the telephone companies join forces to establish a national mobile-free day – an environmentalist gesture similar to oil companies' support of rain-forests.

There are other ways of putting the brakes on as well. For example:

The authorities introduce two half public holidays embedded in office hours, e.g. from 11 a.m. to 2 p.m. This idea was implemented by a Norwegian action group for slowness on 7 June 2000. Workers were encouraged to leave their offices and enjoy a few slow hours with colleagues. It was a considerable success. Seen in isolation, this kind of initiative may seem meaningless, but it is exactly these glimpses of slow time that may be what is needed to stimulate a broad reflection regarding what people actually do with their time. Three empty hours in the middle of the day may offer a sorely needed opportunity to think two, or even three, thoughts through to their logical conclusion. It might even turn out that some of us discover that the world goes on, even if we are taking a long walk instead of being chained to the computer or telephone.

The real purpose of conferences is revealed, namely as pretexts for enjoying some hours or days of slow time with colleagues. As everybody knows, the most important parts of conferences are the conversations that take place during coffee breaks and in the evenings – the people in charge of the schedules must keep this in mind, and compose the programme accordingly. One might even fine those participants whose cellphones ring during the conference (this is already in force in a company of my acquaintance).

Companies establish routine opportunities for slowness during working hours, such as unstructured group talks. In order to give the employees time to take part in this kind of anti-meeting, the management also undertakes to reduce the amount of bureaucratic paper and other thoughtlessly distributed information, to an absolute minimum.

Urban planning is directed towards the architecture of slowness. Open squares, narrow pathways, winding streets and – naturally – beautiful buildings, which encourage passers-by to stop, are prioritised. Slow traffic before fast traffic.

Trade unions must put slowness on the agenda. The trade unions are seen as irrelevant by growing proportions of European wage-workers. This is partly because they grew out of, and still embody, the economy of the Industrial Revolution. If trade unions are going to survive, they badly need revitalisation. If they would put slogans demanding slow time and coherence on their banners next May Day, they might still have a chance. Or, let me put it like this: in October 2000, I was a guest speaker at the national Work Environment Conference in Bergen, western Norway. On the ground floor of the enormous Grieg Hall, there was an exhibition where a large number of companies were allowed to market their solutions to various environmental problems arising at work. Helmets, boots, ventilation systems, ergonomic mice and funny-looking design chairs were amply represented. I kept looking in vain for a company that offered aids such as slowness, coherence and contraptions that would automatically erase unnecessary meetings from people's schedules. The pollution of time and space, more difficult to quantify than the pollution of air and water, is not yet on the environmental agenda.

We are not facing a choice between, on the one hand, the hyperactive, overfilled, accelerated temporality of the moment and, on the other hand, a serene, cumulative, 'organic' temporality. Information technology will for the foreseeable future have a dominant place in our kind of society, and it will affect all – with the possible exception of a small fringe of fundamentalists (that is, people whose identity hinges entirely on what they are against). The project which has been sketched in tentative and doubtless banal ways in these final pages, must consist in finding a balance, that is creating a world which is spacious enough to give room for a wide, inclusive both-and (as opposed to that Protestant principle, either-or). I suspect that, reflecting on their lives on their deathbed some time in the future (whether it is one year or 60 years from now), readers will not regret having spent too little time talking in the mobile phone, writing e-mails, attending meetings, following endless soap operas and moving from A to B – whether by car, plane, taxi or in cyberspace (or, characteristically, all four). When Europeans are asked by pollsters what gives their lives the most meaning, they rarely mention any of these. They do not even talk about vacations in the sun. Most would say 'spending time with close friends', 'watching my children grow up', 'being able to do something for others' or even 'good food' or 'art'. Such answers are not likely to be hypocritical; I believe they should be taken at face value. This book has shown why such values can be so difficult to achieve in practice. Hopefully, it has also indicated that it is entirely possible to have one's cake and eat it too.

Sources

Although books, interviews and other texts published in Scandinavian languages have been used indirectly in the preparation of this book, I do not generally report them below, since they are inaccessible to most of the readers. I should nevertheless mention some important sources of inspiration here. Jon Bing, an Oslo law professor and science fiction writer, has been the most visionary commentator on the information age in Norway for three decades; he is in no small measure responsible for fuelling my initial interest in computers. Trond Berg Eriksen (an historian of ideas, no relation) and Anders Johansen (an anthropologist/media researcher) have both, in very different ways, enlightened me about time in general. Tor Nørretranders, an influential Danish science journalist, has offered crucial insights through his innovative information/exformation contrast, while both Swedish physics professor Bodil Jönsson in her small 1999 book *Tio tankar om tid* ('Ten thoughts about time') and Danish social theorist Lars-Henrik Schmidt converge, in remarkably different ways, with my main perspective on important issues.

2 INFORMATION CULTURE, INFORMATION CULT

Alvin Toffler's *Future Shock* and *The Third Wave*, both of which elaborate on the growing economic role of information – the former on the then contemporary situation, the latter on the near future – were published by Bantam (Toronto 1970) and William Morrow (New York, 1980), respectively. Douglas Adams's *Dirk Gently's Holistic Detective Agency* was published by Pan in 1988. Hobsbawm's *Age of Extremes: The Short Twentieth Century 1914–1991* was published by Oxford University Press in 1994. Baudrillard's statement is *The Gulf War Did Not Take Place* (London: Power Books 1995). Statistics about the number of people online, doubtless updated by the time this is being read, are taken from www.nua.ie. Bringsværd's short story 'The Man Who Collected the First of September 1973', was published in Jorge Luis Borges, Silvina Ocampo and A. Bioy Casares, eds, *The Book of Fantasy* (London: Black Swan 1990). His work in Norwegian is published by the Oslo publisher Gyldendal. Details on Malling's writing ball and Nietzsche's relationship to writing technology is taken from the catalogue to the exhibition 'Hastighet: Det nittende århundre' ('Speed: the nineteenth century') at the Norwegian National Library, spring 2000. Global growth related to various information technologies is well documented in the *UNESCO Statistical Yearbook*; updated information on some issues can be had at www.unesco.org. The Marx quote is from *The Misery of Philosophy* (*La Misère de la philosophie*, 1847 – the only book he wrote in French), a polemic against the French anarchist Proudhon and his book, *The Philosophy of Misery*. The comparison between users of Macs and PCs was described by Edward Mendelson ('How computers can destroy prose', *New York Review of Books* 1990), who refers to a study in Delaware published in *Academic Computing* in 1990. The 'Held et al.' from Figure 2.2 is David Held et al., *Global Transformations: Politics, Economics and Culture* (Cambridge: Polity 1999). Castells is quoted from *End of Millennium* (Oxford: Blackwell 1997), p. 336.

3 THE TIME OF THE BOOK, THE CLOCK AND MONEY

The number of sources used in this chapter can be quantified accurately as something between nothing and several hundred volumes. Overviews of cultural history are rarely uncontroversial. The very idea that human history can be periodised according to major 'watersheds' or great divides, is deeply contested. Personally, I nonetheless draw inspiration from studies such as Jack Goody's books about the state and literacy, the most accessible of which is *The Domestication of the Savage Mind* (Cambridge: Cambridge University Press 1977), and Ernest Gellner's *Plough, Sword and Book: The Structure of Human History* (London: Collins 1988). Marshall McLuhan's *Understanding Media* (1964) has been perused in the Routledge edition of 1994, and it is a remarkable, sparkling book about writing and other 'extensions of the senses'. The anthropologist in Java was Olaf Smedal at the University of Bergen. Henri Bergson's doctoral thesis, *Sur les données immédiates de la conscience*, is currently published in English as *Time and Free Will: An Essay on the Immediate Data of Consciousness* (Minneola, NY: Dover Press). Georg Simmel's *Philosophie des Geldes* was first published in 1907 (current edition Frankfurt: Suhrkamp 1989) exists in English as *The*

Philosophy of Money (London: Routledge 1978), and remains one of the best studies of the communicative significance of money. My colleague Henrik Sinding-Larsen first called my attention to the importance of musical notation. The printing press was elected the most important invention of the last 2,000 years by a group of well-known scholars in diverse fields, see www.edge.com or John Brockman, ed.: *The Greatest Inventions of the Past 2000 Years* (New York: Simon & Schuster 2000). Benedict Anderson's *Imagined Communities* was published in London by Verso (2nd edition 1991). Estimated literacy figures from Elizabethan times are quoted from R.S. Schofield: 'The Measurement of Literacy in Pre-Industrial England', in Jack Goody, ed.: *Literacy in Traditional Societies* (Cambridge: Cambridge University Press 1968).

4 SPEED

The Börretzen quotation is from a CD, *Noen ganger er det all right* ('Sometimes it's all right') (Oslo: Tylden 1995). The theatre diva in question is Wenche Foss, who probably ranks among the five most famous people in Norway. Kundera's *Slowness (La Lenteur)* was published by Faber (London) in 1996. On the plague in the 530s, see David Keys, *Catastrophe: An Investigation into the Origins of the Modern World* (London: Arrow 2000). Virilio is quoted from his interview book *Cybermonde: la politique du pire* (Paris: Textuel 1996). Virtually all of his books can be read as exemplifications of (if not introductions to) dromology. On the issues at hand, his *The Information Bomb*, published by Verso in 2000 (French original 1998), is indispensable. General introductions to Tönnies, Simmel and other classic sociologists abound; a popular textbook is Anthony Giddens's *Sociology* (Cambridge: Polity 1989/1997). The *Scotsman* journalist is quoted after *The Economist*, Millennium Issue, December 1999. James Gleick's *Faster: The Acceleration of Just About Everything* (New York: Pantheon 1999) is the source for the Coca-Cola slogan (p. 50). Hamsun is quoted from *Om det moderne Amerikas Aandsliv* (1889, Eng. ed. *The Cultural Life of Modern America*, Cambridge, MA: Harvard University Press 1969), while Kipling's essay 'American Notes' was first published in 1891 (quoted from the Internet). Paul Virilio writes about photography, film and time in several places, see e.g. *The Vision Machine* (Bloomington: Indiana University Press 1994, orig. edn 1988). The story about Erlander is related by political scientist

Ulf Bjereld in 'Tiden och den fria viljan' ('Time and free will'), *Moderna Tider* ('Modern times', Swedish journal), April 2000. Ramonet's *La Tyrannie de la communication* was published in Paris by Galilée in 1999; he covers the loss of credibility among journalists on pp. 60–1 and the growth rate in information on p. 184. The political scientist who looked into the acceleration of political speech was Ulf Torgersen. The *New Scientist* feature on i-mode and other electronic communications of the present and the near future was published in the 21 October 2000 issue.

5 EXPONENTIAL GROWTH

Malthus's *Essay on The Principle of Population* exists in many editions, and was published in six revised editions in Malthus's own lifetime. Mine is the Oxford University Press version from 1993. Schwartz is quoted after Gleick: *Faster*, p. 188, while the skyscraper example later in the same chapter is taken from the same book, p. 24. Engels introduced the dialectics of nature in an unfinished work, published many years after his death under the title *Dialektik der Natur* (1927, Eng. edn *The Dialectics of Nature*, New York: International Publishers 1940). The Tsembaga are famously described by Roy Rappaport in *Pigs for the Ancestors* (New Haven, CT: Yale University Press 1967), and the story about the polyploid horse is told by Bateson in *Mind and Nature: A Necessary Unity* (London: Wildwood 1979), pp. 66–7. Data on book publishing and paper consumption is taken from the *UNESCO Statistical Yearbook*, 1999. Figures from Amazon.com are taken from the company's annual report, available at www.amazon.com. The growth in intercontinental telephone lines is described in David Held et al., *Global Transformations*, p. 343, while the same book reports on the cuts in transatlantic telephone costs on p. 170. The total number of minutes expended on global telecommunications is quoted from Ramonet, *La Tyrannie de la communication*, pp. 176–7. Statistics on mobile phones in Norway come from Telenor, the main national telephone company. The development in international air traffic is presented at the IATA web site, www.iata.com. Statistics on the development of tourism in the Mediterranean area are taken from Orvar Löfgren, *On Holiday: A History of Vacationing* (Berkeley: University of California Press 1999), p. 251.

6 STACKING

The standard study of *Dynasty* is Jostein Gripsrud, *The Dynasty Years: Hollywood Television and Critical Media Studies* (London: Routledge 1995). Borges' fable on the library of Babylon is published in *Ficciones* (Madrid: Alianza Editorial 1971); in English in *Labyrinths* (London: Penguin 1970). McLuhan's *The Gutenberg Galaxy* was published in 1962 (Toronto: Toronto University Press), but his most influential book was *Understanding Media* (New York: New American Library 1964). Among those who regard his optimism as difficult to understand, we must count some of the most important critical media analysts, including Arthur and Marielouise Kroker, Jean Baudrillard and Paul Virilio. Bill Martin's book is *Listening to the Future: The Time of Progressive Rock 1968–1978* (Chicago: Feedback 1997), and quotations are from pp. 290 and 292. Eno's book is *A Year with Swollen Appendices* (London: Faber 1996), while Castells is quoted from *The Rise of the Network Society* (Oxford: Blackwell 1996), p. 463. Regarding Bourdieu's *Sur la télévision* (1996), I have used the English edition (*On Television*, London: Pluto Press 1998). Galtung is quoted from the manuscript to his *Johan uten land* ('Johan with no land'), Oslo: Aschehoug 2000.

7 THE LEGO BRICK SYNDROME

Recommended texts by the theorists in questions are Jean Baudrillard, *The Illusion of the End* (Cambridge: Polity 1994), Anthony Giddens, *The Constitution of Society* (Cambridge: Polity 1984) and *The Consequences of Modernity* (Cambridge: Polity 1990), Paul Virilio, *From Modernism to Hypermodernism and Beyond*, ed. John Armitage (London: Sage 2000) and Manuel Castells, *The Rise of the Network Society* (Oxford: Blackwell 1996). The full title of Sennett's book is *The Corrosion of Character: The Personal Consequences of Work in the New Capitalism* (New York: Norton 1998). See also Ulrich Beck, *The Brave New World of Work* (Cambridge: Polity Press 2000). The *Guardian* report about work and stress is quoted from *Guardian Weekly* 26 October–1 November 2000. The article about psychoactive medicines is Randolph Nesse: 'Is the Market on Prozac?' www.edge.org/3rd_culture/story/100.html. Bateson wrote about flexibility in a number of articles, most of which are contained in *Steps to an Ecology of Mind* (New York: Bantam 1972). Lasch's *The Culture of Narcissism: American Life in an Age of Diminishing Expectations* was originally published by W.W. Norton in 1978, and continued to be widely read and discussed well into the 1980s. The American edition of Linder's book is *The Harried Leisure Class* (New York: Columbia University Press 1970). Daniel Bell's book is *The Cultural Contradictions of Capitalism* (New York: Basic Books 1978), while Bauman's *Life in Fragments* was published by Blackwell in 1995. Data on speed and slowness in American car culture are taken from Gleick: *Faster*, p. 124f.

8 THE PLEASURES OF SLOW TIME

Michael Ende's *Momo* was published in German in 1973 and in English under the title *The Grey Gentleman* in 1974, before the title was changed to *Momo* for the paperback edition by Puffin in 1984. Giddens's book, *A Runaway World* (actually six radio lectures) was published in London by Profile in 1999, and an unusually bad-tempered attack on his upbeat 'third way' ideology is Pierre Bourdieu and Loïc Wacquant: 'La Nouvelle Vulgate planétaire' (*Le Monde Diplomatique*, May 2000). Habermas's *The Structural Transformation of the Public Sphere*, translated into English only in 1989, was published in paperback by Polity in 1992. Both Peter Cochrane and the two children are quoted from *Little Book of the Millennium* (London: Headline 1999). Lévi-Strauss's book was *Les Structures élémentaires de la parenté* (Paris: PUF 1949; English translation 1969).

Index

Compiled by Auriol Griffith-Jones